EL CAMPESINO

EL CAMPESINO

General El Campesino

EL CAMPESINO

LIFE AND DEATH IN SOVIET RUSSIA

by Valentín Gonzalez
and Julian Gorkin

Translated by Ilsa Barea

G. P. Putnam's Sons   New York

COPYRIGHT, 1952,
BY INTERNATIONAL PRESS ALLIANCE CORPORATION

Library of Congress Catalog Card Number: 52-5275

Manufactured in the United States of America
Van Rees Press • New York

EL CAMPESINO

I

I GREW UP in a hard school. I come from Estremadura, and Estremadura is one of the most backward provinces of Spain. Next to the great estates and the untilled land, which used to belong to the grandees, live peasants without land and often without bread. It is a thankless struggle to wrest a living from that harsh soil, broken up by steep, wild mountain ranges. And it has bred a race of men who are rough, willful, and stubborn: men of action. Most of the peasants of Estremadura could neither read nor write, but they had character and personality. They had pride and a fierce belief in human dignity. In the era of Spain's great conquests, Hernán Cortés, conqueror of Mexico, and Francisco Pizarro, conqueror of Peru, both came from Estremadura.

Such is the region from which I come. I was born in a tiny hamlet, to one of the humblest families. My name was Valentín González. But I carried it only for the first fifteen years of my life. In a country where the revolt against oppression and authority never ceases, rebels develop early.

[3]

My father, Antonio González, launched me on my road. He was an anarchist by instinct, a born rebel. He came from peasant stock, but was first a road maker and later a miner in Peñarroya. Like so many Spaniards, he was impatient of restraint, hostile to authority, and a believer in direct, violent action. Also, he had an ardent desire for justice and a feeling of solidarity with his fellow workers which made him ready to sacrifice himself for the good of all.

My early years were spent in an atmosphere of ceaseless struggle against the oppression of the monarchy. The most bitterly hated servants of the regime were the civil guards. Between them and ourselves there was war to the knife. On their side was all the power and the resources of the government, on ours nothing but the will to fight for freedom.

It has been said the name by which I am known, *El Campesino*, "The Peasant," was given to me by Russian agents at the beginning of the Spanish Civil War, as a trick to win the sympathies of peasants and land workers. This is not true. The name was given to me by the Spanish police on my first arrest, because I took the part of the peasants during a strike. I was fifteen at the time. My name was earned fairly, and I have not dishonored it since.

At sixteen I won my first victory over the civil guard. There was a strike in the coal mines of Peñarroya which spread to other industries and to trade. Strikebreakers were brought into the district. The strikers fought to keep them out; the civil guard protected the blacklegs. It was a tough, violent struggle. Hatred became murderous.

I wanted to strike a real blow. In this I was inspired not only by my father, but also by a leading terrorist called *El Degollado*, "The Cutthroat." It was easy enough to get hold of dynamite in the mines. I made a bomb.

The civil guard had set up a post between one of the factories and the railway embankment. This was my target. Because of the frequent heavy rains of Peñarroya, the hut was raised above the ground by props, like a man on stilts. I decided to put my bomb underneath and blow up the post.

My comrade in the venture was another young terrorist known as *El Virulento*. He was two years older than I. We set out in the night under a bright moon. By creeping along in the shadow of the houses we managed to reach the post unseen. Then we planted our bomb and made off. We had not gone far when we heard a terrific explosion. The bomb destroyed the hut and killed four civil guards. Nobody grieved for them, not in those days and in that place.

El Degollado told us to go to Córdoba and stay in hiding there; he let us have some money for it. But I remembered the advice my father had given me: "If you're on the run, take to the hills. Money will betray you; civilization will betray you; women will betray you. The mountains never will."

El Virulento and I hid in the small hill village of El Hoyo. Thirty hours after the explosion, the civil guards arrested my father. They beat him unconscious, but he swore he had no idea where I was.

We were in a hill district famous as the hide-out of "noble bandits," of men who robbed the rich and helped the poor. We lived like bandits ourselves. We were outlaws, hunted men in spite of our youth, and there was a price on our heads.

The mountains never betrayed us. Nor did the people of the mountains. Peasants sent us food through the shepherds who climbed the steep slopes with their flocks. We used our shoelaces to make snares for rabbits and partridge. In this fashion we lived for seven months. From time to time we left the hills during the night to go down to Peñarroya or another little town. But we risked leaving our shelter once too often. We were just trying to board a goods train at Peñarroya when seven armed men, four of them civil guards, surounded us. They first marched us through the streets, then they beat us up and threatened us with torture unless we led them to the headquarters of the secret terrorist committee. We refused.

In the prisons of Peñarroya, Córdoba, and Fuente Obejuna, they tortured us to make us betray our friends. They beat us with heavy whips. They crushed our feet in a vise. They tightened the handcuffs on our wrists till the circulation was stopped, and left us so for three or four days on end.

El Virulento's spirit resisted their tortures, but his body did not. He died in jail from his sufferings. It was the end of a short and hard life. He had been an orphan, without family or relations. Half bandit, half revolutionary, and wholly a terrorist, he died before he really started to live.

His death was not quite in vain. It brought me my freedom. The lawyers who had undertaken our defense used his death to throw the whole blame on him. They got me free.

I found that I had become a sort of hero among the workers or peasants. The peasants proudly repeated the name the police had given me: El Campesino, the peasant. And I was proud because they were proud of me.

During the months I was in the prison of Fuente Obejuna, my cellmates were anarchists. What I learned from them strengthened me in my political beliefs and in my firm will to fight oppression by every possible means, including violence. It encouraged me even more that peasants sent me food while I was in jail. As soon as I was released, I took up the fight again. I stayed in Peñarroya —illegally—and became the leader of a band of *pistoleros*, gunmen who were out to harass the enemies of the people.

[7]

Then the war in Morocco broke out.

Under the monarchy, the Spanish Army was violently unpopular. This became worse when the army was engaged on a violently unpopular war. The regular officers of the Spanish forces in Africa maintained discipline by treating their men with the same brutality with which they treated their enemies, the Moors.

I shared the people's hatred of the army, the military caste, and the Moroccan War. By then I had reached the age when I was called up for military service. The police detained me and handed me over to the unit for which I was destined. I deserted at the first opportunity. They tracked me down, arrested me, and took me to Seville together with other deserters. There were many like myself who had no intention to fight for the monarchy against which they had been battling all their conscious lives. I deserted again. When I was rounded up for the third time, they took no chances with me. They kept me in handcuffs till after our landing in Ceuta, when they delivered me to my unit at Larache.

My record as a deserter did not recommend me to my sergeant, Suárez. This man was a common criminal who had gone straight from Málaga jail to the Spanish Army in Morocco, thanks to a law which reprieved convicts with prison sentences of less than ten years if they enlisted for five years. Suárez not only insulted and beat

the soldiers in his unit, he made them fight each other
for the sake of his fun. He showered punishments on us
without rhyme or reason. His men hated him. He hated
me. He hated me because I did not cringe before him.
It made him see red that I was not afraid of him. One
day when the company had formed, Suárez ordered "El
Campesino, step forward."

I stepped from the ranks. He strode up to me and,
without saying a word more, slapped my face with all
his might.

I didn't move. I said, "Sergeant, you aren't strong
enough to knock me down."

He roared, "Silence! Step back!"

I knew what I was going to do, but I bided my time.
If my revenge was to be complete, it had to be planned
in such a way that I avoided punishment. One night the
Moors attacked Larache. The skirmish gave me my
chance. I killed Suárez. My officers and my comrades in
the ranks suspected me—but what proof could there be
about a death in battle? After that day I noted that my
officers took care not to be rude to me. And the other
soldiers became more friendly.

They fed us badly at Larache, and one day our pa-
tience gave out. A group of us, myself at its head, broke
into the kitchen and destroyed such stocks of food as
there were. I was locked up. They told me I would get
at least six years in the fortress of Cádiz. But in fact this

incident brought me, not into military prison, but into the ranks of the Communist Party.

I believed myself alone, abandoned, and friendless. Then Joseito came to see me. He was in the navy, but his duty took him to and fro between Cádiz and Larache with supplies for the army. He brought me tobacco and food to eke out the prison fare. Best of all, he found an officer in the Army Legal Corps who had liberal ideas, took on my case, and worked so well for me that I was set free after fifteen weeks.

This was the beginning of my friendship with Joseito.

It turned out that Joseito knew about my history and my political ideas. Now he undertook my further political education. I had read nearly all the important books and pamphlets of Spanish Anarchist literature. Joseito gave me Communist books and periodicals to read.

We Spaniards, and especially we of Estremadura, are individualists. Anarchism comes more naturally to us than communism. But little by little Joseito replaced my individualistic notions with the collective doctrines of the Communists. He roused my enthusiasm for the Russian Revolution. He convinced me of the need for a Communist Party and International, with disciplined members who were willing to sink their personalities in the common cause and obey orders from above without a question. The grandeur of the Bolshevist Revolution overwhelmed me. I felt that Spain, too, was ripe for revolution. And I asked Joseito, "What can I do?"

It was decided that I should start a secret antimilitarist paper under the title *Bandera Roja*, "Red Flag." Joseito was going to direct its policy, but I was to be responsible for it and distribute it among the soldiers.

"A real Communist," Joseito explained, "must do his work, and get others to work, without getting caught. It's up to you to show that you deserve the Party card."

I made the army pay for the costs of the paper which attacked it: I pinched army supplies, sold them, and used the money for the production of *Bandera Roja*.

Joseito taught me that the Moors were right to defend their independence against the Spaniards who had invaded their land. I was not hard to convince. And when I am convinced, I act. As soon as I was disembarked at Alhucemas, with French and Spanish units, I made contact with two Moors and began to supply them with arms and ammunition.

Later on, when I came back to Larache, I went to see the captain who had been my counsel in the food mutiny case. He said, "Take a bit of advice from me. Get out of here—and quick!"

"Why?" I asked.

"You've had dealings with the Moors, haven't you?"

"Maybe."

"They know about it," he said. "You may be arrested

any moment. And this time I wouldn't be able to get you off."

I had entered Larache in uniform. I left it in civilian clothes which my counsel got for me. He also let me have a map of Morocco. At night I crossed the frontier into the Riff, and was at once arrested by the Moors who took me for a spy. It is a wonder they didn't shoot me at once. I told them about my collaboration with the two Moors, and for seventeen days they dragged me all over their territory, trying to find the two men who could confirm my tale. I was lucky. We found them, and the Moors accepted me as their friend. They gave me a horse, arms, and Arab clothing. I lived among the Berbers, sharing their everyday existence and adopting their ways. There is much Moorish blood in Spain, and I must have my share of it. I looked sufficiently like a Moor to pass for one of them.

At the end of the Riff War, the Madrid Government decreed an amnesty for offenders of my sort. I could safely go back to Larache with the Spanish prisoners of war whom the Moors now released. But the army had no use for me. My record had convinced my superiors that I would be more dangerous for them as a soldier in the ranks than as an enemy. Yet in spite of the amnesty it did not seem wise for me to return to Spain as a civilian with the papers I carried. They did not give me a clean bill.

Luckily I found a sergeant with an exemplary service record, who had six children to feed and needed money. He sold me his papers, and so I was equipped with an unblemished character. I made straight for Madrid.

This was the year 1929. I reported at the headquarters of the Spanish Communist Party. The Party considered that I had earned my membership card. I became a member in due form. Then I started work as a road contractor. I kept as much of my earnings for myself as I needed for urgent necessities. The rest I handed over to the Party. I was a full-fledged Communist.

II

THEN CAME the Civil War.

On July 18, 1936, news reached Madrid that the military caste had risen in arms against the Spanish Republic.

When I look back on the day that followed, I wonder how it could have held so much bloodshed and battle, and how I could have seen so much of it. I was among the Republicans who stormed the Cuartel de la Montaña, the barracks which the Fascists had turned into their fortress. Later I joined the fighting for the airfield of Cuatro Vientos. And in the end I found myself with governmental forces operating in the town of Guadalajara, thirty miles from the capital.

And then came another nightmarish day. General Mola was reported to be marching on Madrid. I rounded up some twenty men, and we went to the mountain pass of Somosierra, the key point where Mola had to be stopped if he was to be stopped at all. It was my first command: twenty-nine men, two lorries, rifles, and one machine gun. I did not know it then, but this was the beginning of the famous Forty-Sixth Division, the "Cam-

[14]

pesino Division," the largest formation of shock troops in the Spanish Republican Army. But at the start our group did not carry my name. We adopted that of Chapaev, the great guerrilla fighter of the Russian Revolution. Thus we set out, not even in uniform, with our single machine gun, meaning to stop General Mola's regular soldiers. Fortunately we were not left alone. A column under Colonel Cuerva—who was killed two days later —joined us soon. Then Captain Galán, an active Communist who constituted himself my military adviser, put four hundred men under my command. It was not exactly a strong force to pit against trained soldiers, but it was enough. We beat Mola's troops back and not only made three hundred prisoners, but also took ammunition and lorries which were badly needed. Madrid was saved.

I had a head wound and was sent to a hospital. But I could not stay there idle while the fighting was going on outside. After two days I went back to my post, though it was another month before I could get rid of my bandages.

For my services at Somosierra I was given the rank of captain, in front of my unit in formation. The Communist Party were determined to profit by the distinction I had won; at the ceremony in Buitrago, the members of the Central Committee and even a representative of the Comintern were present.

I heard that the Fascists had captured Villavieja and

held my brother a prisoner there. I moved on Villavieja, took the place back, and freed my brother. This feat brought me the offer of another promotion. I refused. As a lifelong antimilitarist I hated the officers of the army and all they stood for. My new rank of captain was quite enough.

Galán disagreed with me. He had been made a colonel in the meantime, thanks to one of those rapid promotions of the Civil War, caused mainly by the lack of high-ranking officers on our side. Galán wanted me to accept higher rank, possibly because he wished to see the higher command in the hands of Communists. Whatever the reason, he called two thousand militiamen together and proposed my promotion to them. By acclamation they voted me a major and the officer commanding the sector of Buitrago. This was a nomination by the fighting men themselves, and I accepted it.

Almost in spite of me, my command was growing. On August 6, Largo Caballero visited us, confirmed my rank on behalf of the government and—more important—provided uniforms for my militiamen. Now they really began to look like soldiers.

Galán urged me to make an appeal to the Castilian peasants, asking them to join the militia. I had doubts about it. If they had not risen already in defense of the Republic, why should they rise if I called them? Yet so it was. Nobody was more astonished than I when thousands of peasants responded to my appeal and volunteered. Why did they do it? Because they hated professional soldiers as much as I hated them, and would not listen to their appeals, not even to the appeals of those who had remained loyal to the Republican Government. To me they listened because they knew I felt as they did. Because I was El Campesino, the peasant, one of them.

With the peasant volunteers I organized seven battalions. We had barracks of our own in Madrid. I used professional soldiers who had remained loyal as instructors and advisers, but I still did not trust them as leaders. They were with us now, but before that they had been soldiers, and therefore against us—wasn't our enemy in the field the military caste?

The war was going badly for us. From the start the Fascists had the help—solid, substantial help—from the Italians and Germans. We got no help from the Russians until two months after the outbreak of the fighting, and even then it was not on the same scale. And we did not get it for our own sake. But I did not see that at the time. I should have seen it, but I did not. I was blind.

Again Madrid was in danger. On November 4, Largo Caballero, the premier, who prepared for the transfer of his government to Valencia, asked General Miaja and myself to save the city. I took six battalions and posted them at the most dangerous and vulnerable spots.

The decisive days were November 6–9. But many

people in our own camp did not realize that they might be decisive, because they had given Madrid up for lost. The world expected the fall of Madrid from one hour to the next. And the world should have been right; Madrid was ripe to fall. It should have fallen, if the men, women, and children had not united to save it, as no civilians had ever united in defense of their homes.

I am no talker; I am a doer. This time I had to talk. We held a mass rally in the largest theater of the capital, and I spoke to the crowd. I told them, "Stop crying. The Fascists won't enter Madrid. But if we want to stop them, you must turn out, all of you, men and women, children and old people, and dig trenches, and build fortifications round the town. People of Madrid, arise!"

We went out in lorries and collected everybody we found in cafés, theaters, and in the streets. And they came. They worked the whole night with an enthusiasm and a will to resist that might have shamed the government which had abandoned its capital.

The enemy expected to take Madrid on the tenth. Early that day, while I was inspecting the outposts with two of my officers, I saw two Fascist tanks coming up. We captured one of them, the other turned to flight. The lieutenant who commanded the captured tank carried plans for a simultaneous attack on Madrid from nine directions. Forewarned as we now were, we could meet the Fascists at every point. They were surprised by our resistance and withdrew. For the second time Madrid was saved.

     *   *   *   *   *

The Russians had begun to play their game in Spain.

There was the famous Fifth Regiment. All the Communist and more-or-less-Communist writers, journalists, and poets praised it to the skies. They called it unique, and it was unique.

From the beginning, it had been a Communist regiment. But for the first two months of the war, before the Russian intervention, it had been a regiment of Spanish Communists. Then it was a unit of militiamen. Its commander was Major Barbado, member of the Central Committee of the Party. Its political commissar was Enrique Castro. Like so many other old-time Communists, Castro was disillusioned by Moscow at a later stage; he has published a book which explains why he lost faith in Russian Communism.

One of the first steps after Russia began to take a hand in the Civil War was a change in the command of the Fifth Regiment. The Communists replaced Barbado by Lister, who was a typical Stalinist, always putting Russia first and Spain second—or perhaps nowhere. Like Modesto, the second of the two men on whom Russia mainly relied during the Civil War, Lister was Moscow trained in every sense. To complete their control of the Fifth

[19]

Regiment, the Moscow Communists also used two leaders behind the scene. One was Major Orlov, personally delegated by Stalin, and the other, Major Carlos J. Contreras. Nowadays Contreras is known under another name; he is Vittorio Vidali, leader of the Communists in Trieste.

The Russians sought to establish the supremacy of reliable Communist detachments over all the military forces on the Spanish Republican side, through the Fifth Regiment, and also through the International Brigades which they controlled with the help of the Frenchman André Marty and the Italian Longo, who called himself Gallo in Spain. They saw to it that the Fifth was the best equipped regiment, and had ample funds, and that it enjoyed the advice and instruction of Russian technicians as well as of other foreign specialists operating under the close control of Russian agents. The Fifth Regiment was practically independent of the Defense Ministry. For that matter, it was practically independent of the Spanish Republican Government.

The Communists succeeded in terrorizing the professional soldiers who served with them. Those who played the Communist game were rewarded with promotions and glorified by the Communist press in Spain and abroad. Those who showed opposition were discarded, unless they had very strong political support. An example was the case of General Miaja. At the beginning he held out against the Communists; it was decided to remove him from his command. Then he learned of his danger and submitted to Communist direction. At once the Communist press made a favorite of him. Other officers took this object lesson to heart.

In spite of Russian determination to keep the Fifth Regiment under the control and direction of Moscow-trained leaders, it was made part of my command on the orders of Largo Caballero, with the approval of the Russian military advisers. My first shock brigade had been organized at Alcalá de Henares and included six battalions plus two companies of guerrillas. The Fifth Regiment was nominally added to this command. It was done at the time when the Russians made most of me, using my popularity with the masses they had not been able to reach otherwise. Ilya Ehrenbourg wrote a series of articles about me, in which he called me "the Chapaev of the Spanish Revolution." Eventually my brigade became the Forty-Sixth Assault Division.

The arrangement by which the Fifth Regiment was in my command, but under the orders of Lister, offered more advantages to the Russian-trained Communists than to me. They were in a position to get the credit for my victories and let me take the blame for their blunders. For instance, when I took the Cerro de los Angeles, the Communist press celebrated it as Lister's victory. In fact, what he had done was to lose the position and retire to Perales de Tajuna, where he consoled himself by feasting. I had the job of regaining the ground he had lost; and then he emerged once again to reap the credit.

During that time the Russian agents, working mainly from the headquarters of the International Brigades at Madrid and Albacete, organized the execution not only of people who opposed the Communists directly, but also of those who showed reluctance in following their directives. And because the Fifth Regiment was on paper part of my command, they could pile the responsibility for a great number of those acts on me. They found it useful that the name of a commander who was a prominent Communist should inspire terror, behind the lines as well as at the front—and that this man was someone who did not belong to their inner circle. They looked further into the future than I did. I had been brought up in a school of terrorism. I did not shrink from violence. The reputation which was built up around my name did not bother me—then.

I am not pretending that I was not guilty of ugly things myself, or that I never caused needless sacrifice of human lives. I am a Spaniard. We look upon life as tragic. We despise death. The death of a bull in the ring, the death of a man in war, seems a fitting end to us. We do not torture our consciences about one or the other. Throughout the Spanish War, I held power over life and death in my hands. I do not say that I always used it wisely or even justly. I do not apologize for anything I have done.

It was a bitter war. It was not pretty on either side. But Republican excesses, such as they were, were nothing compared with Franco's. It was Franco who mobilized Moorish troops against his countrymen, and gave them free rein. And the excesses of which I may have been guilty myself were nothing compared with those of the Moscow Communists. I did not slaughter my comrades in arms for disagreeing with my political opinions.

Once the Communist caucus used me as a cover and made me arrest one of our supporters. This was when they thought Madrid lost. Modesto and Miaja called me in and told me that the colonel commanding the assault guards of the national palace—the former royal palace— had revolted against the government, and his men with him. This was astonishing news, for the assault guards, a body formed by the Republican Government in 1931, had been constantly loyal to it, in contrast to the reactionary civil guards. But I had no reason to doubt what Modesto and Miaja told me. At their request, I took some men with me and arrested the colonel and his guards. Then I handed him over to Modesto. Only later did I find out that there had been no such thing as a mutiny or revolt. The colonel's only fault was that he was neither a Communist nor the tool of Communists.

This incident left me in control of the royal palace, which had been the residence of Alfonso XIII. I found it disappointing, in spite of its enormous size. It lacked the magnificence I had expected. With my aides I went into the king's bedroom. It was decorated with splendid mirrors and gilt woodwork. Its chief piece of furniture was a huge screen. Across one of the walls stood the king's bed, also gilt, eight feet long and six feet wide, and in a recess above its head was a great crucifix.

"Well," I said to my aides, "who wants to sleep in the king's bed tonight?"

They seemed frightened by the idea, as if they felt a vague superstition. One of them said openly that it would bring bad luck.

"All right," I said, "in that case the bed of the king is for me."

And that night, El Campesino, the peasant, slept in the bed of Alfonso XIII, the last decadent sovereign of what had once been one of the most powerful empires of the world.

He had owned a very comfortable bed.

III

A MORE SIGNIFICANT story is the story of Teruel, and I have to tell it.

At the time of the Fascist rising, this important Aragonese town fell into the hands of the rebels. General Sarabia won it back for the Republic towards the end of 1937. It was a victory of more than military importance. Republican morale had fallen low at this period, and the recapture of Teruel gave the people new faith and new courage.

It also gave renewed prestige to the Socialist leader Indalecio Prieto, under whose orders as minister of defence the action had been carried through. The Communists did not like this. Prieto was no pawn of theirs and stood in their way. While he remained at the head of the Defense Ministry, with his influence undiminished, they could not hope to gain complete control of military affairs. Thus they set out to torpedo Prieto, at the cost of losing Teruel.

The first step was to remove General Sarabia. As long

as he commanded at Teruel, nothing could be done. Not only was he the man who had worked out the campaign for recapturing the town, and therefore the last to risk its loss, he was also a faithful friend of Prieto. The Communists managed to get Sarabia transferred elsewhere, and at the urgent request of the Russian Generals Gregorovich and Barthe, Modesto was made commander in his place. Then they began to put their plot into practice. The advanced defense positions of Teruel were held by Anarcho-Syndicalist divisions. These units were denuded of artillery. Without heavy guns, they could not possibly hold out; they were sure to be driven back from their positions. Teruel would be lost. But the Anarcho-Syndicalists as the troops immediately responsible, and the Socialist Prieto as the minister of defense, would be discredited—at a price.

Though I did not quite see through the scheme, I was not stupid enough to miss the point of the steps which had been taken. I asked Gregorovich, "What is it you're trying to do? liquidate the popular front? Do you really think we Communists are strong enough to hold out by ourselves?"

"It's not a question of liquidating the popular front," Gregorovich answered, "but of making it do what we want. We've got to discredit the Socialists and the Anarcho-Syndicalists, and show people that the Communists are the only ones who can hold Teruel."

I protested, but Gregorovich and Modesto reminded me of the discipline of the Communist movement. And I obeyed. I still had not grasped the full extent of their plans. Because I was not Moscow trained, they did not consider me safe enough to be trusted with them. I knew they were risking Teruel, but thought it was nothing worse than a miscalculation. Only later did I discover that not the endangering but the actual loss of Teruel was a necessary part of their campaign to discredit and discard Prieto.

Their campaign also included my own removal.

It was not that I had earned the hostility of the Russian Communists by that time. I had not. They were still giving me great publicity as a Communist hero, and continued to do so long after Teruel. But I didn't belong to the inner circle. I was a Spaniard, even if I was a Communist, and never forgot it. I was not devoted to Soviet Russia above everything. I sometimes talked back. They used me while my work served their ends. If ever my death were to serve them better, they would be able to spare me. Now they felt that my death would serve them better.

At the beginning, they had used the name of El Campesino to rally the peasants. Later, they had used it to build up fear and terror. Now they intended to use El Campesino to provide a martyr for the cause. Communists have never underrated the importance of martyrs.

Unfortunately for me, fortunately for them, I would have made a good martyr.

The Anarcho-Syndicalists had to be driven back to compromise them; Teruel had to be lost to compromise Prieto and the Socialists. But the Communists had to be the last defenders of the town—this would add to their prestige. So I was left with my men to defend a forlorn hope to the last. If we all were killed, if I was killed, the Communists would be able to blame Prieto for the loss of Teruel—and for the loss of El Campesino. Modesto and Gregorovich had decided that I should render this final service to the Party. The only thing was, they failed to inform me of it.

The Fascist offensive against Teruel, directed by Franco in person, lasted from January 21 to February 9, 1938. The advanced positions were lost, and I quickly found my force of 16,000 men surrounded. Outside the town, Lister and Modesto commanded six brigades and two battalions. They could have helped me. They did nothing of the kind. Even worse, when Captain Valdepeñas wanted to come to my rescue, they prevented him from doing so.

But I have little taste for martyrdom. I fought back. Shut up in Teruel, besieged and encircled by the Fascists, my men fought on splendidly. Of the nine hundred men of my One Hundred First Brigade, who bore the brunt

of the attack, only eighty-two survived. I decorated all
of them when the battle was over.

At the last stage, fighting was going on inside Teruel
itself, around the bull ring. All the nearby buildings were
in ruins. In these ruins, the Fascists were intrenched on
one side, we on the other. I was directing the defense
from a cellar.

Then word was brought to me that the Fascists were
shouting across to our men, "El Campesino is dead—surrender! We've killed El Campesino—surrender!" I ran
out of the cellar, jumped on to the rubble which was our
parapet, and shouted, "Where are those bastards who say
El Campesino is dead? Here I am! Do you think I look
dead?"

The Fascists were so surprised that they did not even
remember to fire at me. Then my aides got hold of me
from behind and pulled me back just in time. The bullets
started whistling overhead just as they hustled me back
into my cellar.

There was no hope of holding Teruel any longer. Now
the task was to try to save my men and as much as possible of our equipment. We fought our way out, through
the encircling forces, at the cost of a thousand men.

Among our casualties was one of my aides. He fell
at my side, killed instantly. I wanted to save his body
and took it on my back. But I soon realized my folly and
laid the body down in the snow. My cloak was soaked

with his blood. I threw it away. This act gave rise to the second report of my death. My cloak was of a special pattern, made for me in Madrid to look like those the Russians wore. My men recognized me by it in the field. Also it had the stars of a commander in chief.

This cloak was picked up and brought to Franco. He called in newspaper correspondents and showed them the bloodstained cloth and the identifying stars. The report went out: "El Campesino is dead." Even the Republican Government believed it. An official telegram informed my wife that I had been killed in action.

As soon as I had led the survivors of my command to safety, I rang up Prieto. "El Campesino speaking," I said. "I've broken out of Teruel with most of my men and a good deal of our material."

"You're joking," said Prieto. "El Campesino is dead. Who is that speaking?"

"Go to bloody hell," I started, but Prieto interrupted me: "Now I recognize you," he said. "I know you by your vocabulary."

When I found out that two hundred guns were available in Valencia and could have been transferred to the Anarcho-Syndicalist units to hold Teruel, I was furious. I demanded that Lister, who had clearly left me in the lurch, be removed from his post. But the Russians protected him and that was that.

Two months later Prieto, whose position had been

weakened by the loss of Teruel, was forced to go—after a Communist mass meeting conducted by La Pasionaria, at which he was accused of negotiations with the Fascists. Dr. Negrín, the premier, took over the Defense Ministry himself. The Russians thought they could manage him more easily than the stubborn Prieto.

And Franco had taken Teruel.

IV

THE WAR was going from bad to worse. It was no longer possible to doubt what its end would be, and this end was very near.

The war cost me my family. My father had organized and led the largest group of militiamen in Estremadura, 12,000 strong. As arms they had what they could get, hunting rifles, pistols taken from civil guards, and home-made bombs. For two months they had been fighting in the region between Salamanca and Cáceres to prevent Franco from getting arms or reinforcements of Moorish troops via Portugal. Then my father was captured. My sister Maria was arrested. The Falangists hanged both of them. It was for my father's exploits that they were executed; but it was because they were my next of kin that their bodies were left hanging for a week, with placards on them announcing triumphantly that these were the father and the sister of El Campesino.

Because the Fascists could not kill me, they killed my wife and my three children. All the men of my family were wiped out, and all of the women, except one cousin.

My younger brother, who fought like a lion in the war, was taken prisoner—I cannot understand how, being my brother, he let himself be taken alive! When they were through with him, they shot him. I was fatal to all those who were related to me.

✻   ✻   ✻   ✻   ✻

At the beginning of the disastrous war, when we had a very different vision of its end, Colonel Francisco Galán and I had sworn not to shave until the day we entered Burgos, the capital of Franco. I had grown a thick, black beard, not long, but tightly curled. It was not well groomed; we had no time for beauty treatments in our campaigns. But it had become my hallmark, a distinguishing feature by which I was recognized everywhere.

With defeat upon us, a distinguishing feature became a bad thing to have. It was obvious that we were not going to enter Burgos. Galán shaved off his beard and advised me to shave off mine. I said I would. It so happened that some ardent Communists in Galán's command saw him without his beard and questioned him about it. He told them that I was going to follow his example.

A little later I was called to the Central Committee of the Communist Party in Madrid "on urgent business." It never occurred to me to connect the summons with my beard, and I went. When three Russian generals backed by La Pasionaria urged me not to sacrifice my beard, I thought they were pulling my leg. At first they spoke with a grin, joked, and compared my beard to Samson's mane. But when they saw that I would not take them seriously, they all became very grave and earnest. To my amazement I found that the "urgent business" for which they had called me away from my post consisted in that beard of mine. They told me that I had to keep it; it had become legendary. If I shaved it off people would take it as a bad omen. A clean-shaven Campesino would no longer be El Campesino.

One of the Russian generals said, "Your beard isn't your personal property. It belongs to the Spanish people, to the Revolution, to the International. You have no right to shave it off. It is a matter of Party discipline."

They even made the Secretary-General of the Party, José Díaz, ring me up during our conversation, to convince me of the "political importance" of keeping my beard. I kept it.

I kept my beard until Valencia. We were still resisting at Valencia, but we knew that our only hope was to hack our way out and reach the coast elsewhere. My aides believed that my chances would be better if I got rid of that easily identifiable beard. But I refused to cut it off. I had promised to keep it, and I repeated to them what the Russian generals had told me.

My aides had no respect for the wisdom of Russian

generals. They grabbed me, tied me to a chair, and tackled my beard. The more I swore at them, the more they roared with laughter. So they scraped off my beard and some of my skin with it. Then they wrapped it up in a piece of paper and hid it under the roof of the house. But first they wrote on the wrapping, "This is the beard of El Campesino. It belongs to the Spanish people. One day we will come back for it."

We got into our powerful car with as many arms as we could handle. Then we roared out of Valencia towards the southwest coast. We had to cross the eastern provinces of Spain and part of the south. Here and there Franco supporters had set up road blocks and control points. But, though the Fascists had won the war, they had not yet managed to establish order. Everything was in wild confusion. The roads were choked with fugitives, civilians and soldiers, some seeking a place where they could hide, others going to surrender themselves.

Without my beard I slipped past at most of the control points. Even so, Falangists recognized me three times and tried to arrest me. We shot our way out with our automatic weapons. Three times our route was marked by the bodies of those who had tried to stop us.

By a miracle we reached the coast, at the little fishing village of Adra, twenty-five miles from Almería on the road to Málaga. The Franco forces had not yet moved in. Adra was still run by a Socialist administrator called

Belmonte. He gave us shelter in his house which also served as the office of the local council of which he was the head.

Night fell. Suddenly the calm was shattered by shots, shouts, the sound of tramping feet, and the clatter of hoofs. The soldiers of Franco had reached Adra.

The Fascist commissioner presented himself at Belmonte's office. We had only just time to hide in another room and lock the door. Through the thin partition wall we could hear the voices of the new administrator, his wife, and his assistants. They had brought a wireless set along, to pick up official messages. Someone turned it on. From our hide-out we listened. It broadcast the message that El Campesino was somewhere in the region. Survivors at the last road block where they had tried to stop us had given the alarm.

The radio ordered, "El Campesino must be taken, dead or alive."

We could hear the Fascists in the next room discussing it. The commissioner gave order to his assistants to post sentries on all the roads and send scouting parties to look for us. "Let's get out of here," I said to my friends.

We burst into their midst, firing as we entered. The Fascists had no time to act. We killed all who were in the room and rushed out into the streets. The noise of our shooting had roused the sentries outside. As we emerged, they opened fire. We returned it even while we were making for the harbor. The running battle went on all the way from the house to the beach. Belmonte's wife was hit and fell. It looked as if she had been killed on the spot, but there was no time to stop and find out. We ran on.

Several motor launches were moored in the small harbor. We picked out the boat which seemed biggest and most powerful, and pushed off. As we were moving away from the shore, we saw our pursuers putting out after us. We ceased our fire so as not to betray our position, and plowed through the black waves without lights. Thanks either to the darkness or to our choice of a boat, we shook off our enemies.

The engine chugged steadily, our bow cut the water into twin fans of white foam. We set our course for Africa.

V

CROSSING THE Mediterranean was not difficult. Our tank had not enough petrol for the whole long passage, but we stopped a fishing boat and commandeered as much as we needed. Turning eastwards—we would have landed in Spanish Morocco otherwise—we followed the African coast to Oran, in French territory. There I at once got in touch with French Communists. They told me that I had been reported dead again. The Spanish radio had announced that I was believed to have been killed. It was quite a reasonable assumption. The Fascists at Adra had no inkling that I was involved in the skirmish there. The last news of me had come from the third control point where we had shot it out. Afterwards—nothing. It was natural to think that I had been killed in the fight.

The wife of the French Communist leader, Maurice Thorez, and two Communist deputies went with me to Marseilles and on to Paris. I was given a triumphant welcome by the Politburo of the Party and by its parliamentary group. One might have thought I had won the war instead of losing it.

It was decided that I should go to Russia. Where else? I was an exile and a Communist. I had nowhere else to go. I had no business anywhere else on the face of the earth. The French Communist officials gave me an endless questionnaire to fill in, as they did to the other Spaniards and members of the International Brigades who were to be sent to Soviet Russia. My comrades docilely answered the innumerable questions and recorded their private histories down to the last details. I threw the questionnaire back and told them, "The Russians knew me well enough. I don't have to answer all these questions."

The ship which was to take me to Russia was waiting at Le Havre. She was a Russian ship, a combined cargo and passenger boat which normally plied the route from Leningrad to New York via London, and was considered the newest and most luxurious Soviet vessel afloat. This time she had been sent especially from Leningrad to Le Havre to pick up the most important Communist fighters of the Spanish War.

When I came to Le Havre, the official car of the Soviet Consul was waiting for me at the station. It took me straight to the ship, which weighed anchor at once. She had been waiting for me; all the others were on board. We sailed on May 14, 1939.

There were about three hundred and fifty passengers: more than half the Politburo and the Central Committee of the Spanish Communist Party, the commanding officers of the Fifth Regiment, and some thirty leaders of the International Brigades.

With us came the famous Soviet writer Ilya Ehrenbourg. I had met him in Spain and had not liked him. He had spent most of the Spanish War in the most elegant hotels, had driven round in the most expensive cars, and all at the expense of the Spanish people. Officially he was nothing but the most brilliant war correspondent of *Pravda*. But his intimate contact with the Russian Army and G.P.U. people in Spain made me suspect that he had other, less straightforward missions as well.

Perhaps I ought to have been grateful for his flattering articles, but I wasn't. For one thing, he had published a story of my life which was full of blatant falsehoods. And then his oily, theatrical, and jesuitical ways annoyed me. I tried to keep out of his way on board, but he seemed to stick to me like a burr. In a sugary tone and a half confidential, half patronizing manner he began to give me good advice. I had to consider myself as subject to the discipline of the Communist International and not to that of the Spanish Party. Because of my role in the Civil War, I stood a good chance of being regarded as the chief of the Spanish immigrants in the U.S.S.R., provided I showed that I had a clear grasp of my position and its limits. The true and only fatherland of Communists all over the world was the Soviet Union, and our indisputable head was Comrade Stalin.

I remember that I answered him hotly, "I'm a Spaniard above all and will always be. Anyhow, I don't intend to stay in Moscow for more than a few months. Then I'll go back to Spain and organize the guerrillas."

He shook his head sadly, and explained that I would have to get my impulsive temper and self-willed character under control if I wished to be a good Communist. Then he added, "Now you must begin to study, get a good political and military training, and carry out the wishes of our leader." His words alarmed me, and I asked him a few questions about the Soviet Union. In a mild tone he said, "You'll have to prepare yourself for a shock when you see what things are really like. You foreign Communists have been idealizing the Soviet Union. Socialism isn't perfect yet. There are still many weaknesses and failures—and many enemies and saboteurs."

"Do you mean to say the Soviet paradise isn't any such thing?" I asked naïvely.

With an ironic smirk he answered. "The 'paradise' is a propaganda invention. After all, why should other peoples learn the truth?" He finished by saying gravely, "Spain lies behind you. The Soviet Union is now your only country. Don't forget that. And above all, don't start any discussion."

Ehrenbourg must have known very little about the

Spanish mind. He certainly didn't know me. All that his words achieved was to make me feel suspicious and curious. For the first time I asked myself, with a feeling of oppression and fear, what might be waiting for me in Soviet Russia.

I tried to get information from the leaders of the International Brigades who had lived in the Soviet Union before. They had been my good friends and comrades in arms. Most of them were Germans who had gone to Spain to fight against Hitler there, and they had felt happy to do so. They had warmly responded to our Spanish directness and plain speaking. I thought they would tell me the truth. But I found them quite changed; they were depressed, fearful, or suspicious, but in any case inaccessible. It was more than clear that they resented my questions and did not wish to talk. Only those who had not been to Soviet Russia before counted themselves lucky to go there; the others sounded worried. It was as if they felt the blow of having lost the war more deeply than we Spaniards—perhaps because they knew how failures are regarded in the U.S.S.R., whatever their reasons. There was a wall between them and myself, which I had never noticed before.

Only one of them dared talk with me. He was a veteran German Communist who had done well in our war. He had been classified as being an "anarchist" and "undisciplined," and had volunteered for service in Spain to

clear himself of those black marks. He was going back
to Soviet Russia because he had left his wife and two
children there as hostages. He told me that most of his
comrades were in the same situation. He was under no
illusion; from the moment he stepped aboard he knew
himself in the power of the N.K.V.D. Only when there
was no one in sight did he talk frankly to me, and even
then he kept his voice low.

It was this friend who first told me about the working
conditions and the life of peasants and industrial workers
in Russia, and about the regime, its bureaucracy, police,
and terror. When I reacted violently to some of the things
he said, he warned me, "You're a good Spaniard but an
undisciplined Communist, and you're going to pay for it.
Even you who come to the Soviet Union with a great
name and great fame! Will that save you?" He shook his
head. I answered, "I want to find out the truth, and I
don't mind paying the price."

* * * * *

Our ship landed us at Kronstadt.

As soon as she entered harbor, two small launches
came alongside and N.K.V.D. men swarmed aboard,
some in uniform and others in plain clothes. They started
at once a thorough search of our luggage. Each passenger
was called in separately. Everything of the least value
was confiscated, even books, periodicals, photographs,

and personal letters. I had nothing with me but a small bag with toilet things. "Here we've a real revolutionary general!" one of the agents exclaimed. The words were approving, but the tone betrayed disappointment. Perhaps he was sorry because I did not bring all the gold and jewelry which the Franco radio said I had taken with me from Spain.

My Spanish comrades emerged from their ordeal with an air of sad bewilderment. They did not protest. Not the careful search itself stunned them, but the rudeness of the N.K.V.D. agents in dealing with Communist refugees who were, after all, not quite unknown persons. I think we all began to feel that nothing belonged to us any more, that we did not even belong to ourselves any more.

Another kind of welcome was staged for us at Leningrad. The port was decked with enormous posters bearing the portraits of Stalin, Molotov, and Beria. Beneath milled a crowd whose shabby clothing I noticed even then. In an immense, barnlike structure in the port, long tables were set out, loaded with flowers, savories, cakes, and bottles of wine and vodka. They had sent a delegation from Moscow to receive us—representatives of the government, the Comintern and the trade-unions. A Colonel Popov presided. There were toasts and speeches translated by a Russian interpreter whom I had known in Spain two years earlier. I was called upon to say something. I said we had come to the Soviet Union to heal our wounds and to find solidarity for our task of liberating the Spanish people. A Russian replied in the name of Stalin that the Soviet Union welcomed us as its guests of honor and would place each one of us at the battle post to which we were entitled. Our spirits rose, helped by the good food and drink. Here was comradeship! We cheered Stalin, the U.S.S.R., and the future revolutionary Spain.

Afterwards Colonel Popov came up to me, with the interpreter at his elbow. From the beginning he had singled me out for special consideration. Now he was friendly, brotherly, and flattering. "General, we regard you as the foremost representative of our Spanish comrades. I hope you will help us to know the others better, so that every one gets the job for which he is best fitted. Can you give us detailed information about them?"

My face must have registered my feelings, while I stalled in my answer. Popov insisted smilingly, "We trust you absolutely. What we want is to know our comrades thoroughly so that we don't make any mistakes with them. You're a great Communist fighter. You should have every interest in making our task easier."

The interpreter gave the last sentence a slight hint of menace. I was not forthcoming. Popov became even more urgent, and also more precise. He demanded information about all those who had come on our ship—their behavior during our war, their remarks, if any, about the Moscow trials, and their personal characteristics. I parried the questions as best I could. I was sure he meant to check my reports against the statements in the questionnaires my comrades had filled in, and against the answers he would get from others. It also might have been a way of testing me.

After the ceremony, we were driven to the railway station. What I saw on our way through Leningrad was depressing. Side by side with great modern factories were miserable hovels. Popov, who kept observing me closely, wanted to know what I thought. I asked him why they hadn't built houses fit for workers to live in, if they had been able to build those marvelous industrial plants. He answered coolly, "All this is a transition. What is important for the Soviet Union now are the factories."

Leningrad Station was jammed with people. Many were lying on the floor among their packs and bundles, in the greatest filth. When our group came in, some of them pressed towards us in lively curiosity. At once a group of N.K.V.D. militiamen drove, pushed, and kicked them out. I spoke my mind to the interpreter who stood beside me. He, who had known me in Spain, answered, "Here in the U.S.S.R. you can choose between two things: the best places to live in, or Siberia. I can see you haven't changed. But you'll have to change yourself completely here—or you'll have a very bad time."

In the train we were divided into three categories. Each group was sent to the class of coaches which, in the opinion of the Russians, corresponded to its rank and importance. Pullman cars were reserved for top-ranking military leaders like myself, for the prominent members of the Central Committee, and, of course, for the fifteen delegates who had come from Moscow to meet us. These delegates and the interpreter were the only ones who had the right to move freely from one coach to another. We others were allowed to go to the restaurant car—once. In the Pullman cars we could order drinks and cakes. The lesser ranks elsewhere had to go without these delicacies.

The whole train was in the charge of N.K.V.D. guards, although it carried only Communists who had passed the hardest tests. They did not let us leave the train at any of the stations where it stopped, not even to stretch our legs, and no one was allowed to get in. We were given strict orders what to do and what not to do during the journey, including the hours in which we might smoke. We were caught in the iron discipline of the Russian Communists.

At Moscow we were received as no other foreigners had been received before, or so I was told. At least fifty cars and a horde of journalists, photographers, and officials waited for us at the station. I, in particular, was greeted by an outburst of publicity. My photograph appeared everywhere. I was in all the news reels. Press and radio magnified what I had done. I was the hero of the hour. But when I wanted to walk through the streets of Moscow and look at things with my German friend who was my inseparable companion, four N.K.V.D. guards went with us everywhere. They had worked out an itinerary for me. I did not care to see Moscow in that fashion and stopped my wanderings.

The living quarters they allotted to me were beyond complaint. Along with the others who had been deemed worthy of a seat in a Pullman car, I was put up at Monino House, a luxury establishment quite different from anything I had expected to find in Soviet Russia. I had my first surprise when I went to the baths to get rid of the dust of the journey. My German friend came with me. Two pretty young girls, more elegantly dressed than any of the women I had seen in the streets, showed us into the bathroom. I waited for them to go out, but they stayed. At my question, my friend told me that they were there to soap us and look after us. I was ashamed at the thought of undressing before them and letting them help me with my bath. But my friend whispered, "Don't protest and let them do their job. And see you drip Communism from all your pores all the time—remember, every word and every gesture of yours will be noted down."

Every refugee of rank had a servant maid to himself, all of them young, well dressed, and perfumed. They carried the membership card of the Komsomol and were a feature of Monino House.

Monino House had a main building, which stood in a great park planted with pine trees, and twelve bungalows surrounded by gardens full of flowers. Rowing boats were moored at a wharf running out into the river. The social center of the Monino was the dining room with its huge windows looking onto the park. It seated a hundred persons. There were flowers on each table, in Soviet Russia a great luxury. The kitchen provided the special dishes of several nations. Wines and liqueurs were freely available. And all this was served by pretty, smiling, young waitresses, who spoke several languages and knew the art of provocation, both erotic and political. Their principal duty was to make themselves agreeable to us. A *maître d'hôtel* used to stand in the center of the dining room and see to it that none of the waitresses made a mistake. A weekly meeting was reserved for complaints or criticism of the service. Our waitresses knew that any complaint would bring punishment upon them.

The private maids of the Monino's more important guests were there to obey our slightest wish and do any service for us, including that of going to bed with us. They did it so naturally, so much as a matter of course, that it seemed an elementary duty. It was as easy to ask them this "service" as it was to ask them to wash up; only they did it with more alacrity. This was, after all, what their masters of the N.K.V.D. wished them to do, for a man is never so prone to speak his innermost mind as when he is with a woman with whom he has shared the ultimate intimacy. Even in their moments of transport, in what should have been their moments of greatest tenderness, these girls never forgot to listen for a word of criticism or revolt which they might pass on. In this way new arrivals in Moscow were observed and catalogued for the first time.

I stayed three months at the Monino, leaving its confines only when I was taken to a meeting or a public function. My German friend stayed only two months.

He had told me of his fear that he was still branded as "undisciplined," even though he was lodged at the Monino with the other prominent members of our group, and that one day he would be called for. His greatest worry was that he had not been allowed to get in touch with his family after his return to Moscow. His wife did not even know he was back in Russia. If he were to disappear there would be no one to inquire for him.

One day he failed to turn up. I asked if anyone had seen him. Two of his comrades told me that a car had come to the Monino at eight in the morning and that they had seen him get in. He had left no message for me.

I asked the manager of Monino House what had happened to my friend. He smiled and said, "He's been sent on a mission." Then he gave me a look and added, "Comrade, in the Soviet Union you must never ask where someone has been sent on work for the Party or the Comintern."

I ignored his hint and asked everyone who was at all likely to know whether there was any news of him. Nobody knew anything. I never heard of him again.

VI

AFTER THREE MONTHS' leisure at the Monino, I was sent as a student to the highest staff college in the Soviet Union, the Frunze Academy.

It was not my own choice. What I wanted was not to be taught how to be a Red Army general, but to re-enter Spain illegally and start organizing the guerrillas against Franco. But I did not decide for myself. My fate, and that of all the others who came to Russia from Spain, was in the hands of a special committee in Moscow. It consisted of five Spaniards; La Pasionaria, her secretary Irene Tobosco, Modesto, Lister, and Martínez Cartón (who later was sent to Mexico to direct the assassination of Trotsky; the Frenchman André Marty; the Italian Palmiro Togliatti; and the two Russians, Bielov and Blagoieva, who were leading members of the Comintern and the N.K.V.D. They resolved that I should go to the Soviet training school for generals.

I protested against their decision to José Díaz, the secretary-general of our Party, whom I knew better than any of the committee members, and whose task it had therefore been to inform me of my allotted role. Díaz said, "You have been one of the bravest soldiers we had in the war, but now you must study modern scientific warfare. The Frunze Academy is the best military college in the Soviet Union, and possibly in the whole world. You'll learn a lot there."

"Do you really think so?" I asked. "I wouldn't expect it, not when I think of the officers the Russians sent to us in Spain."

He gave me a friendly warning, "Don't be so quick to criticize, and be a bit more moderate when you say what you think. They don't like that sort of outspokenness here."

This talk settled nothing. It took three or four sessions before I gave in. I repeated again and again that my place was not in Russia but in Spain, and that I wanted to get there as quickly as possible.

Once he answered me, "But you can't go to Spain. You have no papers."

"I only need the papers to get out of Russia. Once I'm outside I'll manage the rest," I said.

He didn't tell me what I learned later on, that it was precisely the permit to leave Soviet Russia which would have been denied me. On another occasion he tried to persuade me that the standard of living of the Russian workers was higher than that of the Spanish workers. From what little I then knew about wages and prices I thought he was wrong. I pointed out to him that it was enough to look at the clothes and faces of workers in the streets of Moscow to guess at their situation. In the end he admitted, "You may be right, but don't let us go into it now. Once we're back in Spain, we'll try to build up real socialism, different from things here. But for the moment keep quiet and obey orders."

With José Díaz it was at least possible to talk frankly. He was a simple man, honest and sympathetic, though he was no great political, intellectual, or military leader. And he certainly was no match for the old foxes of the Comintern. He talked me round by promising that I would stay in the Frunze Academy for eight months only and would be permitted to go abroad afterwards.

There were twenty-eight of us Spaniards selected for training at the Academy, and in addition four Russian women who had worked in Spain during the Civil War. These women were admitted to the Academy together with us so that they should be able to carry on their old assignment of spying on us. Apart from us, the only foreigners studying at the college were thirty-two Chinese officers. After we left, the only other exception as far as I know was made for officers of the satellite countries at the end of the World War.

The Chinese officers were listed and passed off as Mongolians, citizens of the U.S.S.R. We Spaniards were passed off as Russians.

During my first week at the Frunze Academy I had no name, only a number. We spent that week studying the military code, particularly the sections dealing with discipline and its sanctions. We also heard about the privileges and benefits of being an army officer in the U.S.S.R. At the end of the week uniforms and official papers were given to us. This ceremony was attended by a general who represented the Soviet Government, by the chairman of the board directing the Academy, and by its C.O. When my turn came, the general handed me my papers with the words, "From now on your name is Komisaro Piotr Antonovich."

"My name is El Campesino," said I. "I am proud of it. I don't wish to change it."

With a sour smile he answered, "Whatever your name has been, it is Komisaro Piotr Antonovich." And he turned to the next man.

I never discovered who had hit upon that name for me. But I made a protest to the Spanish Party leaders. La Pasionaria told me, "The name of El Campesino isn't your property. It belongs to the Party which gave it to you."

"It never did that," I said. "I was El Campesino long before I ever joined the Party. I earned the name at my own risk with my own blood, and I mean to keep it."

They called me to the room of the officer commanding the Academy. Sternly he said, "Komisaro Piotr Antonovich, you are an officer of the Red Army now; you are under Communist military discipline. If you maintain your rebellious attitude, you will have to be court-martialed in accordance with the military code you have been studying."

I could do nothing. Henceforth I was Komisaro Piotr Antonovich to the Russians. I was formally forbidden to use the name of El Campesino again. My re-education began with the loss of my name. It was meant to put an end to my past and to my identity as a Spaniard. The other Spaniards at the college had their names changed in the same way and for the same purpose. Apart from the psychological reasons there was a practical reason as well. Our presence at the Soviet Staff College was a military secret. The world was not to know it.

We had nothing to complain about our position inside the college. We not only got the pay corresponding to our respective ranks, but also the emoluments to which our decorations from the Spanish War entitled us. The majority of our group ranked as brigadiers; three—Lister, Tagüeña and Merino—as divisional commanders (generals); I myself as general commanding a mobile shock division (a category by itself); and Modesto as general commanding an army corps, a post he had held at the end of the Civil War.

Modesto and Lister had to go through a special training, both military and political, to prepare them for operating in France, if and when the situation favored a Communist triumph in the neighboring country of Spain. Tagüeña was being trained for a similar job in Hungary; Merino for Czechoslovakia. Merino actually went to Prague when the Communists came to power there. If I was intended for a definite assignment, I never heard of it. Probably they had not made up their minds, because I had not exactly given proof of my capacity for discipline.

The highest pay was Modesto's and my own, 1,800 rubles a month. This was very much indeed. Our instructors, who all held ranks from colonel to general, were paid from 1,200 to 1,900 rubles. The C.O. of the Academy himself got no more than 3,000 rubles. And the average monthly earnings of workers in Moscow ranged from 250 to 300 rubles! If I had continued my military career in the U.S.S.R. through the World War, my pay would have reached 5,000 rubles a month. In addition, we enjoyed the privilege of all price reductions, special services, and services free of charge in respect of food, rent, travel, entertainment, medical care, and so forth.

Even within our privileged circle there were gradations and distinctions. Thus we were all entitled to eat in the restaurants of the Academy at special prices; but there were three different dining rooms, each for a separate category of people. The best was for the use of the teaching staff and the "international generals," the second best for high-ranking Russian officers, the third for the rest of the students. They gave us the finest food imaginable, sometimes dishes it would have been hard to get elsewhere for love or money. And we paid ridiculously low prices. A steak that would have cost a normal person outside 20 rubles—which a worker certainly could not have afforded on his wages—cost us less than a ruble, 90 kopek.

Our prestige, too, was well looked after. No opportunity was missed to refer to us as the "Comrades International Generals", and to remind us that we were "the highest military category of International Communism," the future "leaders of the Red Army in the service of World Revolution." When they mentioned Spain, it was only to bring it home to us that there we had been at the head of a miserably weak and small army, while we now were preparing for posts of command in the glorious Red Army of our great leader, Stalin.

A building dedicated to the "Heroes of the Russian Revolution," and nearing completion at that time, was thrown open to us. As each room was finished, we moved in one by one. I happened to be the first Spaniard to get quarters there. Apart from ourselves, the Russians who had fought in Spain and some who had fought in Mongolia, China, and other countries were allowed to live there. The rooms were exceptionally large, up to seventy-five feet long, and usually destined for two families, with a kitchen and a bathroom. The building was some eight hundred yards from the Academy proper. Its neighbors did not appreciate its presence, because it was guarded by the N.K.V.D. with extreme care. People living within a radius of two hundred yards needed a special pass signed personally by Beria, the chief of the N.K.V.D., to be able to get into their own homes.

The Frunze Academy occupied one of the largest and most modern buildings of Moscow. It also had a great number of branch establishments, "polygons," training and testing grounds for the various arms, most of them close to the capital. Only the center for gas warfare was at a distance of some hundred miles from Moscow. During my own stay, from August, 1939, to January, 1941, between five and six thousand officers were studying at the Academy. A panel of generals, about a hundred of them, prepared the courses, inspected and supervised the college. The teaching staff and other personnel were at least twice the number of the pupils. All our professors had Russian names and Russian ranks, like the students, but many of them were foreigners. It was easy enough to spot them even when they spoke Russian without an accent. Though they wore Red Army uniforms, they wore no decorations. The Russians were aglitter with them; some wore up to twenty ribbons. Also, each foreign teacher had two secretaries with him during all his courses, who were apparently there to help with the maps.

I myself knew the following foreign instructors: two Italians, one ranking as general, the other as colonel, both infantry; one French general; two English generals; two Chinese colonels; one Mongolian colonel; two Estonian generals; four Germans engaged on hush-hush work, three of them generals and one colonel. I met one of them later in Tashkent where he had been deported.

Among our artillery instructors were two by the name of Zhukov. One became the famous marshal who entered Berlin.

We were supposed to know nothing about the real nationality of our teachers. It was the rigid rule of the Academy that we were to confine ourselves to our own courses and our official relationship with our instructors, and never to try to discover the real identity of either teachers or fellow students. If we were being trained for future service in Europe, we had nothing to do with the officers who trained for service in Asia. As my own account shows, it was impossible to enforce this rule of secrecy with complete success. But the system was very near perfection, thanks to the intricate mutual espionage. In principle we were all informers. We were all supposed to report any fellow student or teacher who showed curiosity about the others or gave too much information. If we failed to report suspicious remarks or behavior, we never knew if we would not be reported ourselves for that failure, because the other person might be an *agent provocateur*. Apart from the N.K.V.D. officials at the Academy who were known as such, there were many others we did not know—possibly the most unlikely people. Of one thing, however, we were quite certain: all the women in the college, secretaries, interpreters, and so on, were in the pay of the N.K.V.D. And they were not the only women whom we met.

Outside the Academy was a large public garden. By the time we left, having finished our day's studies, it was always crowded with attractive, elegant, young women. It was very easy to pick up an acquaintance. In fact, it was easier to do it than not to do it, for the girls themselves used to take the initiative and accost anyone from the Academy. They would describe themselves as students, office workers, or sometimes even as simple working women, which they did not look in the least. Each spoke several languages. Also, each one seemed to have a room of her own, in itself a curious circumstance in overcrowded Moscow. There they would offer us choice food and vodka, which they could not possibly have afforded if they were what they pretended to be. We hardly ever doubted that they were Stakhanovites of love in the service of the N.K.V.D.

Still, our exacting curriculum left us little time for dangerous pastimes. We had to report at the Academy at six sharp in the morning. After twenty minutes of calisthenics, we were put through our drill in goose step for the rest of an hour. Then we had breakfast. At eight sharp every pupil had to be in his class. An unexplained absence or coming five minutes late meant the lockup. The Academy had its own prison for minor offenses committed within its four walls, and a disciplinary board with powers to punish infractions of the rules. But these infractions had to be slight indeed to be treated as a domestic matter of the college. Absenteeism or lack of punctuality might be within the competence of the disciplinary board a first and a second time. But the third time the offender was deprived of his uniform and turned over to the N.K.V.D.

The courses and lectures went on from eight till four. After each class, which lasted either one or two hours, we had a break of ten minutes during which we were allowed to smoke or drink a cup of tea. The timetable was so arranged that all the pupils went through all the lectures in strict turn. At three the restaurants opened, and we could dine there when our classes were over. But we still had our homework to do; we had to sort out and copy our careful notes from each lecture for inspection on the following day. If they included drawings, these had to be done to scale overnight.

Our technical military training was rigorous and exacting, but to the minds of our instructors it was not so important as our political training. A good strategist who was not a blind supporter of the regime was potentially more dangerous than an indifferent strategist who was, because the first could do more damage if he ever changed sides. The other might commit all sorts of blunders which involved the loss of lives, and he would have to pay the price of failure, but he would always remain a pillar of the regime.

The political examinations worried the students at the Frunze Academy more than any technical examination. The highest mark was five. Those who did not get at least a three, in some cases a four, were immediately expelled, even if they were brilliant in other subjects. An expulsion not only ended a man's career, it also branded him as a suspect character. The higher the military rank of a student, the more was demanded of him in political knowledge and reliability. A brigadier or divisional commander had to have a political education equal to that of a graduate of the Marx-Engels-Lenin Institute. We had to know the history of the Communist Party such as it was officially taught at the time. We had to master the minutest details of Stalin's life as a political and military leader. No, as *the* leader. For, the figure of Lenin was overshadowed by Stalin, while Trotsky was mentioned only to demonstrate Stalin's wisdom and farsightedness in undoing Trotsky's incessant errors and acts of treason. And then we were taught to see every problem under the sun in the light of Stalinism and to believe that he, Stalin, the "greatest leader of all times," was infallible.

Every officer and pupil of the Frunze Academy had to be a totalitarian fanatic.

VII

LIFE AT THE Academy was beginning to irk me. It was not only the obligatory secrecy, the atmosphere of spying, and the demand for political conformity, all foreign to my nature. There was also the feeling that I, who had always fought oppression of the people, was being turned into an oppressor myself; that I, who had no use for any sort of caste, was now a privileged member of the military caste. To make it worse, this military caste tended to become hereditary, as far as I could see.

During my eighteen months at the Frunze Academy, I knew only four fellow students who had been manual workers. Two of them had so distinguished themselves as soldiers that they were first promoted to the rank of lieutenants and later admitted to the staff college because of their outstanding military gifts and proved devotion to the regime. Two others, one of them a former miner from Stalinogorsk, the other a former metal worker, had made their way there through the N.K.V.D., through their services against "counterrevolutionaries" during the great purge. But once inside the college, these

[65]

four ex-workers found themselves regarded as upstarts and outsiders. One of them spoke Spanish. He began to tell me about it.

Confidences were rare in our lives at Frunze Academy. But either this man turned to me because of my reputation for outspokenness and lack of discipline, or because he had to talk to someone and did no longer care whether he chose the right person or not. He knew what threat was hanging over him. Twice he had been called before the disciplinary board of the Academy. He realized that the next time other people would deal with him. His mouth was twisted in a bitter smile all the time. It was he who told me many things about the working of the Academy, the histories of some other students, the true nationality of our teachers, and so forth.

He told me one day, "Sooner or later we workers will all be expelled. There have been workers here before, and they've all disappeared. The others hate us. They denounce us whenever they can. There's a class struggle within the college. The ones who came from the privileged classes look down on us; they think we have no right to posts of command in the Red Army."

He was right. One after the other, all those four who had been workers left for Siberia.

But what this man had said to me made me observe the social class from which my fellow students were drawn. It was, of course, different with the foreigners who were in an exceptional position. Yet nearly all the Russian student officers were the sons of important officials, of engineers or factory directors, or of army officers. The sons of officers constituted a special group. The military themselves were interested in reserving the high posts to their caste; the regime found it useful to reward the fathers by promoting the sons and so tying both to its service.

The real inner circle, however, was formed by the sons of officials who had helped to consolidate Stalin's regime by their activities against anarchists, kulaks, Trotskyites, Bukharinites, etc. Because of what they had done, the survival of their fathers depended on the survival of the regime; the sons enjoyed an exaggerated respect at the Academy—unless one or the other individual was found to be unworthy of his father by one of the countless informers.

I had been admitted to this select company because of my past services and because I was a foreigner. But I did not feel happy in it.

✿   ✿   ✿   ✿   ✿

During all this time my private worry and tension was eased by the devoted affection of a young woman.

While I was still fighting in Spain, the Soviet press had published the news that I had been decorated with the order of Lenin by the Russian Generals Gregorovich and Malinovski (who called himself Manolito then). Shortly afterwards I had a letter from the Komsomol congratulating me. It was signed Ariadna Nikolaia. I answered it as one answers that sort of letter. It did not seem very likely then that I would ever meet Ariadna Nikolaia. But one day while I was staying at the Monino, I went to the International Library to look up the files of Spanish Communist newspapers. A young girl who studied Spanish was there too. She recognized me from my photographs and introduced herself, Ariadna Nikolaia.

She was fair-haired, a trifle taller than I, very young, very intelligent, and very pretty. I learned that she was studying for an engineering job. She belonged to the Soviet élite. Her father was an old Bolshevik who had been N.C.O. under the Czar, had worked with Budenny in the Fourteenth Cavalry Corps during the Russian Civil War, and had risen to the rank of general in the Red Army. From that time on he was a friend of Stalin. Ariadna herself was friendly with Stalin's daughter.

A few days later I met her again at a football match. This time I made a date with her. Four months after my arrival in Russia we got married, with the highest official blessing; our witnesses were Gorki, secretary of President Kalinin, and the adjutant of Beria, the N.K.V.D. chief. We lived at first in a room of the small flat of Ariadna's father, then we moved into the annex of the

Frunze Academy I have described. Ariadna was a great help to me, especially in the early days when she taught me to speak Russian, showed me Moscow, and introduced me to people it was useful for me to know.

At the Academy things were going badly for me. I never seemed able to learn that if my examiners questioned me about my opinions, they did not wish to hear what I really thought, but only the opinions I had been told to hold. I ought to have rattled them off like a parrot. But even when I had grasped this fact, I still couldn't bring myself to behave accordingly.

We were regularly subjected to such probings. In addition to the scheduled examinations and outside the normal school hours, we had to go through oral tests every two or three months. It was one of them which marked my final fall from grace.

I was already in bad odor, and knew it. I insisted on regarding myself as a Spanish, not a Russian Communist. I had criticized the way factories and Kolkhozes were run, and had said loudly that such a method would not work in Spain—a frightful heresy! It was being whispered that I, who had fought against the Spanish Trotskyites by every means because I believed I was serving the cause by it, was a secret Trotskyite myself. And there is no deadlier crime in the U.S.S.R. Then came the fateful test.

The examining board consisted of the director of the

Academy, the chairman of the board governing it, and one of my professors. All other Spaniards had been asked, among other questions, which army was the best in the world in their opinion. They all had answered, "The Soviet Army."

I did not think so. When my turn to answer came, I said, "In my opinion, the German Army is the best in the world. It is the German Army we must prepare to meet in battle."

This caused a sensation. It was the wrong answer, certainly not the answer I was supposed to give. But I thought it my duty to answer as I did. If I was right—and I had been in a position to gauge the quality of the German Army!—what I said was important, because it is important to know the extent and direction of a possible danger. I knew that my examiners only wished to find out whether I had absorbed the official doctrine and was willing to repeat it, but the servility of my comrades had disgusted me too much.

A grave view was taken of my reply. I was called before the director, and a special board of interrogation was formed with some other members of the administration of the Academy. They not only fired questions at me, they also tried to convince me that I had been wrong; that, first, the Soviet Army was the best in the world; that, secondly, we had to prepare not against the German Army but against the armies of the "Imperialist

Powers." (The Nazi-Soviet pact was still in force then.)
The director assured me that the armies most dangerous
to the Soviet Union were the British and the French. The
chairman of the governing board interrupted, "Do you
at least understand the meaning of our pact with Ger-
many?"

"I understand it all right," I answered, "but I still think
we should prepare against the German Army in spite of
everything."

The interrogation lasted four hours. Our discussion
became increasingly violent. In the end I was exasperated and became insulting in my tone. When one of the
Russian generals said that Kutuzov was "the greatest
commander in Russian military history," I began to laugh
rudely. This seemed a grave offense to them. But they
still tried to convince me of Soviet superiority over the
Germans by quoting incidents of the Spanish War—about
which I knew more than they did. So I told them, "Every
time we got a tobacco issue for our men, all the Soviet
officers, including the brass hats, tried to grab it. I don't
think that could happen in any other army."

"But why is it you cast doubt on the fact that the Soviet
Army is the best in the world?" cried the director angrily.

"During our war in Spain," I said, "I believed you'd
sent us your worst officers. But since I've come here I've
found out that the rest aren't any better. The officers have
lost touch with the people. All they think of is manicuring

[71]

their nails, learning dance steps, and having good manners so they'll be sent on a mission abroad."

This was bad enough. I didn't make it any better when I was asked, in a lecture on maneuvering, what was the task of a scouting party. I was still boiling with rage, and answered, "In the U.S.S.R., the chief task of scouts is to steal chickens and find pretty girls for the C.O."

It was true, but I oughtn't to have said it.

I was labeled a Trotskyite and expelled from the Frunze Academy. It did not come as a surprise.

*   *   *   *   *

My fault was too grave for the mere negative punishment of expulsion. Something more positive had to be done to me.

Lister and Modesto were the two members of the Spanish group at the Frunze Academy who had to report on their comrades and, if necessary, to denounce them either to the Executive Committee of the Spanish Communist Party in Moscow, or to the Comintern, or to the N.K.V.D. They chose to refer my case to the Spanish Committee. They wanted it dealt with as quickly as possible, through internal disciplinary action, so that it should not pass out of their hands. La Pasionaria and Jesús Hernández, the two most important committee members, backed them. There were two reasons for this. For one thing, they knew my influence among the rank-

and-file of Spanish refugees in Russia; those unfortunates had good reason to complain of the conditions in which they were forced to live, and often wrote to me rather than to the Committee which theoretically represented them. Therefore the Committee feared their reaction against anything they might do to me, and wished to keep the whole affair unknown outside its own narrow circle.

But there was a second, more powerful reason for their tactics. When they attacked and accused me, I hit back. They were afraid of letting any outside body hear what I had to say about them—it might have meant trouble.

Most of my accusations would not have done them any harm with their Russian masters. They were, briefly:

1) The Spanish Communist Party had done its best to smash the coalition of political parties and trade-unions in the popular front, and to replace it by a Communist domination of Republican Spain.

2) The Spanish Communist Party had established a reign of crime and terror in the Republican zone, both at the front and behind it, with the result of weakening the other anti-Fascist forces.

3) The Spanish Communist Party had proved itself incompetent to direct the war, secure a distribution of arms, and feed the civilian population.

4) These facts, for which the Spanish Communist

Party was solely responsible, had helped to demoralize the army and the civilian population and thus made the task of Franco's troops easier.

At that time I must still have retained some faith in Russian Communism, for I believed that these charges of mine would discredit the Spanish Party leaders in Russian eyes. I still clung to the belief that those acts had been local errors, in contradiction with the true spirit of communism such as it had been evolved in Soviet Russia. In reality the Spanish Party had only carried out the directives from Moscow. The Russians had not been concerned with the winning of the Civil War, but with strengthening the position of the Party which was their tool. The members of the Spanish Committee knew this well, even if I did not. They were worried not about my political charges, but about two accusations of a personal character which might involve them in trouble.

I accused La Pasionaria of having contrived the release of her lover, Francisco Antón, from a concentration camp in occupied France, and his transfer to Moscow in a Nazi aircraft at a time when many Spanish Communists with good service records were left to rot as prisoners in France and North Africa. The Spanish refugees in Russia were particularly angry about this because they knew that La Pasionaria's son and her husband, a worker from Bilbao and a fine man, were living in the Soviet Union under the most miserable conditions, totally neglected by her. Later her son was killed at Stalingrad. Soviet propaganda exploited his splendid courage and self-sacrifice to shed more glory on his mother.

I accused Lister of a graver crime. Together with Modesto he had gone to a school at Kaluga on a mission to advance the political education of Spanish refugees, young girls who were pupils there. All he did was to get drunk and rape five of the girls. His excuse was that they were "Fascists." I had in my possession a letter signed by the five victims, which gave the details of this ugly incident.

The Spanish Committee would have liked to deal with me within its own authority and not let those two personal accusations go any further. But I made it quite clear that I would not accept any disciplinary measure without a protest, and the Committee had no executive powers to enforce its discipline against such a protest. They referred my case to the organization to which the Spanish Communist Party was subordinated, the Comintern. The Comintern appointed a special committee to deal with it.

This committee had between twenty and twenty-five members, varying from day to day. I have been told that it was the largest committee of its kind to sit on an individual case. The Spanish Party was represented by La Pasionaria and Jesús Hernández. Among the others were Florin, an old friend of Lenin, and the two N.K.V.D.

agents in the Comintern Executive, Bielov and Blagoieva. The most important Communist Parties were represented. At times Dimitroff, the president of the Comintern, attended the sessions; occasionally even Manuilski, the real power behind Dimitroff. This was clear by the way everybody looked at him when he came into the room and listened when he said a word. Manuilski's opinions were never discussed. They were orders.

To this impressive committee the Spanish Communist leaders presented their case against me. They submitted the reports of Lister and Modesto. They also pressed some of the Spanish refugees, people who used to write to me about their worries and complaints, into sending resolutions which condemned my "constant lack of discipline," my "egocentric behavior," my "anarchist individualism," or my "Trotskyite spirit of criticism and opposition."

La Pasionaria told the committee, "El Campesino has always behaved as an individualist. He would never admit that he was wrong, and now he is again obstinately refusing to admit it. He fails to understand that a single member, no matter who he is, cannot be right when he is in opposition to the International."

I retorted, "You're just a hysterical woman. I'm not a lickspittle like you; I've got my own ideas to defend and I'm going to defend them."

Irene Tobosco, La Pasionaria's secretary and personal

spy, attacked me venomously. Lister, Modesto, and a few more of my Spanish fellow students at the Frunze Academy demanded my detention. I tried to counter-attack, but in vain. Right at the beginning of the investigation I was warned that I should submit myself entirely to the Comintern. At this I told them that I was a Spaniard, a Spanish Communist, and wished to be judged not by the "Spanish Committee," but by the whole body of Spanish Communists living in the U.S.S.R. I demanded that fifty-odd of my comrades should be called as witnesses for the truth of my accusations against the Party's conduct of the Civil War. This was turned down by the special committee. "The Comintern is not a bourgeois law court," I was told.

I had to admit the truth of this.

My personal charges met with no better luck. My criticism of La Pasionaria was simply brushed aside. I seemed to make more impression with my charge against Lister, which I substantiated by showing the letter to the committee. I was asked to hand it over, but refused until I was given a formal promise that Lister would be disciplined. Then I surrendered the letter, and that ended the question. Lister was never disciplined.

The special committee sat for fourteen days, and its sessions never lasted less than twelve hours. The members of the inquisition took turns in cross-examining me. I defended myself badly. Badly, that is, if I wanted to be rehabilitated by this committee. Not so badly, perhaps, if I wanted to defend my individual independence which so shocked those yes-men. I was violent. I shouted and swore at the Spanish representatives. I knew the whole time that my only chance was complete capitulation, complete submission, but this was the one thing I could not bring myself to do.

Every night when I left after a session, I walked past a police van standing ready to carry me off, should the order for my arrest be given. Every night my wife was surprised to see me back home. In the end I was tired. I asked for permission to leave the country. It was a childish thing to ask.

VIII

THE POLICE VAN waited for me in vain.

When I consider what happened to others who had been accused of Trotskyism in Russia, I must admit that the Comintern was very mild in its treatment of my case. Perhaps the reason was that my fame in Russia was too fresh in people's memories to make my public disgrace convenient.

At the last session the committee informed me of its decision. I was given a chance to prove that I was a genuine Bolshevik; I was sent to manual labor on the construction of the new Moscow underground. Good, faithful work and evidence of change of heart might lead to my rehabilitation. It depended on me whether I would one day be allowed to go back to the Frunze Academy without loss of privilege. I was not even turned out of the room in the house dedicated to the heroes of the Russian Revolution, where I lived with Ariadna. A Bulgarian, friend and assistant to Blagoieva and, like her, a member of the N.K.V.D., was appointed to take me to the underground and settle the details of my work there.

The Russians are extremely proud of the Moscow underground. It is their prize exhibit for foreign delegations, journalists, and tourists. They claim it as a masterpiece of construction, and they are quite right. Only, they forget to explain that it is a monument not only to Soviet engineering but also to the slave labor which went into its construction.

Almost 90 per cent of the construction workers were in a position similar to mine. Many of them were old fighters, former military leaders, or even N.K.V.D. men. They had fallen into disgrace and had been allotted this sort of work which offered them the faint—the very faint—hope that their efforts would in time restore them to their former position in the ruling class. It is as easy to fall into disgrace in Russia, as it is hard to climb back to favor. Yet the alternative to this work was Siberia, and so they did all they could to follow the faint ray of hope.

Strictly speaking, I had not been convicted of anything and no sentence had been passed. This did not alter the fact that I was a forced laborer. I had to stay in the job into which I was put, without a possibility of leaving, or even of being transferred to another gang of workers in the underground. There was no promotion of any sort open to me. The N.K.V.D. had listed me as a worker capable of a maximum output. In my first job, which was placing great nuts and bolts with the help of enormous spanners, this classification meant that I had to place 265 a day, while the normal rate was 165 a day. My pride drove me to exceed even that maximum norm, as often as not. The same happened when I was put on work with concrete or when I had to shift soil with a wheelbarrow. But however hard I worked, my pay was always the same: 300 rubles a month, the basic wage of workers in Moscow—a starvation wage. In practice, however, I hardly ever got as much as 200 rubles, when all the deductions had been made.

Lack of modern machinery and equipment made our work very difficult. Human muscles and effort had to replace the missing tools. I often worked in water up to my knees. After some time I noticed that I was always sent to the most dangerous spot when there had been a cave-in. An accident at work would have been a nice way of getting rid of me, I suppose. Then Soviet propaganda would have turned me into a hero again.

I started work in the underground in March, 1941. In June, the Nazis invaded Russia. Our work of eight hours underground, under bad conditions, without the tools we needed, was bad enough in itself. But when the German attack came, we were told that the underground was going to be used as an air-raid shelter and that work had to be stepped up. It sometimes happened that we stayed underground for six days on end, working without a break except for a short nap now and then when we could not go on. At the same time the network of spies and *agents provocateurs* in the labor gangs was intensified. For the mildest word of criticism anyone was likely to be arrested as a "defeatist" within a few hours, and with him all those who had been within earshot but failed to report the remark.

For me personally there was nothing new in this increased espionage. From the moment I started in the underground, I was under special surveillance. It was Ariadna who had first spotted the two agents shadowing me. She happened to see them when she stood at the window, waiting for me to return from work, and pointed them out to me later on. I would see them patiently waiting down in the street while I was upstairs in our room, and sometimes I would get a glimpse of them following me when I went out. They did not seem to mind being recognized. One evening we stayed with Ariadna's father till late and took a taxi home. The driver tried to cheat on the fare and we argued with him. Suddenly my two agents came up, gave us a military salute, and roughly ordered the taximan to get a move on.

Sometimes the methods changed. Once I met three Spanish refugees in the street. They were very friendly and gave me good advice: I ought to give in and inform the Comintern that I now submitted to its authority without reservation. I ought to admit my past mistakes, and then I would go back to my post in the Academy. I told them that I would stop being a revolutionary if I gave in, and that I preferred to go back to Spain with clean hands. Much later, when I was in the Lubianka jail, I found that my words were recorded in the file as a black mark against me.

Then there was a worker in my gang who took to hanging his clothes next to mine. One evening I went with Ariadna to a Komsomol gathering. My mate was there—in the uniform of the N.K.V.D. . . .

❖   ❖   ❖   ❖   ❖

The people of Moscow were shocked and bewildered when the Nazis broke through the lines of the Red Army in five days. After the first three months of the war there was a general feeling that all was lost. In the fifth month there was chaos. Industrial plants suddenly closed and left their workers without instructions, without wages. Some of the factories were evacuated with their machinery, others were destroyed so as not to fall into enemy hands.

A colonel of the N.K.V.D. by the name of Sergeiev came to see me while I was working in the underground, together with another colonel whose name I never learned. They told me I had been chosen to work on a special project. They still considered me an active Communist, despite my disgrace, a man who could be trusted with confidential tasks. With a small group of other workers in the underground, all of them Komsomol members, I was put on construction work in one of the stations between the Red Square and the Krasniye Vorota. We had to build a wall for some mysterious purpose. It was secret work. Exceptional precautions were being taken. The entrances to the station were guarded by N.K.V.D. posts; they let only those of us pass who were working on the wall. Trains were still running, but they no longer stopped at this station. While all the other stations were used as air-raid shelters, ours was closed to everybody, even during air raids.

This extraordinary secrecy naturally made me curious. One day, when Colonel Sergeiev seemed in an especially friendly mood, I asked him lightly, "Now, what is it you're going to hide here—the treasure of the Kremlin?"

He smiled and said, "Yes, the greatest treasure of the Soviet Union. Comrade Lenin."

When he saw my surprise, he put his finger to his mouth and told me with the utmost gravity that I was to keep the secret to myself. I was astonished he had ever let it out. But even in the Soviet Union, people sometimes feel the need to confide in someone. And to the colonel, I was still an important Communist general, even though in disgrace for the time being. Also, I have noticed that Russian Communists occasionally trust foreign Party workers more than their own comrades.

Thus it was in the underground of Moscow that Lenin's embalmed body was hidden while Moscow was in danger of being occupied by the enemy. When the danger had passed, it was taken back to its mausoleum in the Red Square.

As the German armies drew nearer, panic increased in Moscow. The people were clamoring for evacuation, but nobody organized it. Officials and important personages were too busy with their own evacuation. They commandeered all cars, buses, and lorries, and fled. It was every man for himself and the devil take the hindmost.

Some of the things the political leaders said over the radio were anything but reassuring to their listeners. For instance, the secretary of the Komsomol spoke two days running, and said that the regime was in danger, but that this danger had unmasked its enemies who would all be shot one day. Somebody must have decided that his words were not well chosen. He was shot himself.

After twelve days of this muddle and panic Stalin himself broadcast, not from Moscow as was given out, but from Kuibyshev. He spoke in a feeble, sugary, expressionless voice and told people of Russia's acute danger. He called upon them to rise against the invaders and destroy the whole wealth of the country rather than let it fall into the hands of the enemy.

Moscow became a setting for bonfires. In the middle of the Red Square, piles of papers and ledgers were set on fire—the records of the Kremlin. In some of the districts I saw portraits of Lenin being burned in great quantities, and even greater quantities of portraits of Stalin. In all official buildings the few clerks who had stayed on were busy burning papers. Burning had become a kind of mania.

At this stage the guard of the Kremlin itself was taken over by 120 Spanish Communists, students at the Planesnaya School, a political training college. They stayed at their post during the last two days, until they found out that they were guarding an empty shell. Then they too left Moscow.

I could not help comparing this sorry spectacle with that of Madrid on the eve of its siege. And I was proud of Madrid.

As to myself, I stayed at work in the underground until two days before the final great rush from the capital. Then we were told that work was being stopped. We asked for instructions what to do, and were told, "Stay on—get out—do what you like."

The young laborers in my gang threw their arms round me. One of them said, "The government is breaking down. Perhaps we'll never see this Russia again!" Both were members of the Komsomol, but the outlook did not seem to harass them unduly.

I left Moscow in November, 1941, by train. We called it the "crazy train" or the "pirate train." Both descriptions were true. Our train rocked crazily through the country, roaming about in this or that direction, backward or forward, without a definite goal, except that of finding something to eat for the passengers. We, the passengers, were pirates; we used the train as pirates used their ships, to get to the victims we intended to plunder.

The Luftwaffe helped me to a good seat on the crazy train. It would have been a hard task otherwise. On their flight from Moscow, people stormed the trains in wild hordes. The engines were manned by professional engine drivers or by amateurs, and driven off on whatever line led away from the enemy. When I got to the station, German bombers were overhead. I was hardened to air raids by the Spanish War. While most of the people who had been battling for seats ran to the shelters, I settled down in the best seat I could find and managed to keep it even when the crowd returned, and until the train pulled out slowly, bound for nowhere.

Passengers on our train were in a state of riot. They smashed up seats and tore off roofing to get fuel for the stoves in the coaches. We had no food with us and no normal means of getting it, so we stole food. We stopped the train at villages and sacked them. We took potatoes from storage, and roast potatoes were our staple food. When we got hold of flour, we baked bread on the train in some fashion. We stole what we could get and where we could get it.

The "pirates" of the train gave vent to their hatred when they met well-dressed members of the privileged classes with money in their pockets, such as officials or factory managers. Then they would assault them, beat them up, and leave them naked.

The crazy train was nowhere a welcome arrival. If we stopped at a station, its officials tried to get rid of us as quickly as possible. Usually they did it by pointing out another place where we would be sure of finding ample food. On the train there was no law and no authority, but after a time some sort of order was introduced by an improvised committee. I was one of its members. We tried to steer the train on its mad course. The few N.K.V.D. men among the passengers were too happy to be tolerated at all to make any attempt at establishing their lost authority.

On this crazy train I spent a good six weeks. Later I found that it was not the only one of its kind. Sixty such trains were careening about at some stage in Uzbekistan alone. Their passengers, who sacked the countryside, were sometimes sacked themselves. Gangs of armed deserters would hold up a train, drive out all its passengers, occupy it themselves, and force the engine driver to take them where they expected to find something to eat.

In the end, our train left us at Tashkent. There, between one million and one-and-a-half million refugees were crowded together, mostly old people, women, and stray children. It was bitterly cold. Everybody went hungry. Those starving, ragged, exhausted refugees were

mowed down by typhoid. Nobody bothered about bury-
ing the bodies left lying in the streets.

There was plenty of banditry. Groups of thirty to forty
would gang together to protect their miserable belong-
ings. Then a stronger group would loot them of all they
had in the world. And then the first group would "go
bandit" in its turn, and find weaker victims to plunder.
Old women, being the feeblest of the lot, suffered the
most. Younger women usually managed to survive. I saw
women who were naked, and women wrapped in potato
sacks with a hole for the head and two for the arms.
Bandits had taken away their clothes to barter them for a
piece of bread or a few potatoes. Some other women had
pieced odd rags together anyhow. They looked funny and
pitiful. One wanted to laugh and cry at the same time.
The awful thing is that we laughed more than we cried.

MY WIFE HAD gone with her mother to Kustanai in
Kazakstan, where her father was organizing the First and
Second Siberian Divisions. As soon as I had got in touch
with her and could arrange it, I left Tashkent to join her.
But I was no longer free to decide where I wanted to
stay. I was again caught in the mesh of the N.K.V.D.,
and they decided that my forced residence was to be
Kokand in Uzbekistan, near the mountain range of Turkestan. So I had to go there, and Ariadna came with me.

I was not put to work this time, as in the Moscow underground. There were not nearly enough jobs for all
the refugees who had been concentrated in the town. I
met a number of Spaniards, refugees from the Civil War
like myself; only some of them had found work, the men
in a war factory, the women knitting socks and pull-overs
for the soldiers. Their wages, especially the women's,
were miserably low. Like other refugees, I was granted
300 rubles a month by the Red Aid, but only for six
months. Then I had to fend for myself.

A delegate of the Spanish Communist Party was supposed to look after the Spanish refugees in Kokand. He was Rafael Vidiella, a man who had been a counselor of the Government of Catalonia and the representative of the Catalan Communists at the Executive of the Comintern. He was in charge of the distribution of food to the Spaniards, and he certainly did not go short of anything. I made an enemy of him when I discovered that he had stuck a heavy coin on one side of the scales in which he weighed the few ounces of bread he then doled out to the refugees.

The Spaniards were only a small part of the army of refugees in Uzbekistan. The whole territory of the Republic, and the neighboring Republics, were at that time crammed with masses of people of all sorts and all breeds —and all uprooted. They had come following a rumor that the regime had lost control of those regions. There were those who wanted to get out of the way of the authorities for a particular reason, and those who had no personal reason but only shared the general fear of the police and wished to enjoy something like freedom thanks to the chaos. There were deserters, evacuées from factories and Kolkhozes, Poles who had been released from internment camps when the German attack on Russia had turned them from enemies into allies. There were public servants who had left their posts and taken great sums of money with them, and prisoners of war who had escaped from German-occupied countries. There were political refugees of all nationalities, Yugoslavs, Poles, Czechs, Austrians, Germans, Italians, Frenchmen, Spaniards, and so forth; and there were professional bandits.

All fugitives from the Soviet police were barred from legal means of livelihood. Only the public servants had money—the money they had embezzled—to buy what they needed. The others had to find money by whatever means they could. Men became bandits. Women became whores.

It was not rare to see a woman selling herself to a peasant for a chunk of bread or a handful of potatoes. I saw a Spanish woman offering herself close by the railway station where her refugee husband was looking after their child and waiting for her to come back with the money and food she had earned; they were all starved. I heard of wealthy Tartars who were delighted to buy the most attractive European women, women who could sell nothing but themselves. I knew of a married woman who was sold by her own husband for 5,000 rubles. It was cheaper to buy a public official. Identity papers complete with every signature and stamp cost between 20 and 30 rubles.

The N.K.V.D. dispatched one police unit after the other to Uzbekistan to bring order into the boundless confusion. As soon as a new unit arrived, it used to make common cause with the bandits. In fact, the most dangerous bands were led by N.K.V.D. men.

I spent nearly two years in Kokand. Though I was supposed never to move from the city, I made a series of journeys at times when I knew that a close control of travelers was impossible. They were not pleasure trips. I made them for two different reasons, one political and the other purely practical. They corresponded to my divided state of mind.

In those years I was torn between the wish to stay in the Soviet Union and the wish to escape. I felt a burning need to know and understand more about the Stalin regime. I still considered myself a true Communist. It is difficult to break away from a faith into which one has sunk one's whole life, for which one has sacrificed everything and everybody, for which one has even committed crimes, believing them to be necessary for the future of mankind. I thought it would be possible to form genuine Communist Parties outside Stalinist Communism, or even against it. Nearly everybody who has broken away from Stalinism has passed through such a stage of illusion.

Some of my journeys from Kokand were inspired by my wish to learn about the Soviet regime. Others, which I made from June, 1943, onwards, had to do with my plans for escape from Soviet Russia.

During that month I managed to get hold of a considerable sum of money—by illegal means, of course, because there were no others open to me. From one of the many corrupt officials I bought false papers, which I needed for traveling without the risk of being detained, and went to Samarkand. Then I made three consecutive journeys on the railway from Samarkand to the Caspian Sea port of Krasnovodsk. I wanted to study the frontier line between Turkmenia and Persia, because the Russian maps deliberately falsified the frontiers, like everything else. On a piece of paper which I kept carefully hidden I noted—in code—which stations were strongly guarded by the N.K.V.D. and which were least dangerous, also the timetable of the trains and details of the frontier guards. It took me the whole month of August to find out what I needed, but I did find it out.

*   &   *   &   *

I have said that I needed money for those trips, and got it "by illegal means." In 1943 there was only one way for a penniless man in Kokand to make money, by becoming a bandit. I became a bandit.

For this decision I offer no apologies. To survive in the society in which I found myself then, one had to be either a bureaucrat or a bandit. I could have been an army bureaucrat of the highest rank. But I preferred to be a bandit and to deal with other bandits, with prostitutes, and with corrupt officials. Why should I repent of it, when it was the price I had to pay for my life, liberty, and self-respect—though this may sound odd?

The idea of the "noble bandit" is common enough in Spain. Bandits used to be part of Spanish everyday life, particularly in my native province of Estremadura. I had known bandits when I was a little boy—not romantic, legendary figures like the Robin Hood English children read about, but real men in the flesh, who robbed, killed, and lived as outlaws because they would not come to terms with the laws of their oppressors. They were a threat to the civil guard and to the rich; they were no threat to us. They used to protect us in a hundred ways, and sometimes they gave to the poor part of what they took from the rich. In Russia, too, people had a tradition of "noble bandits." There existed something like a bandit's honor in countries where the outlaws alone had never bowed down to oppression.

This does not mean to say that the bandits of Uzbekistan at that time were "noble." They arose when the social order went to pieces and everybody stole from everybody else. The strongest and boldest were the masters, and the strongest and boldest were the bandits. They took what they wanted. What I wanted was money. I took it.

There were countless organized robber bands in the region. They robbed, and sometimes killed people in possession of large sums of money. This meant above all industrial managers, high officials, or Kolkhoze administrators. One of the bands consisted of Spanish refugee children. All over Russia there were packs of homeless, orphaned children who kept alive by stealing and looting. But the exceptional thing about that band of abandoned Spanish children was the way in which they clung to their national identity. They refused to mix with the other homeless children. They even used a Spanish Republican flag as their emblem. I do not know what became of them, only that a few were executed by the Russians. They were not executed as bandits, but as "Falangists"—boys who had been taken to Soviet Russia during the Spanish War, when they were small children!

Among the robber bands at Kokand there was a small group of four led by a man who was held in great fear. This was the one I joined in June, 1943. They had arms and got arms for me. I made good, so much so that I ousted the leader and became captain of the band myself. Of our exploits I remember two which had their funny side. Once we learned that the manager of a Kolkhoze at Kokand, where the workers were starving, had hidden away a large amount of money for his personal use. We took it from him. He found himself in a cleft stick. How was he going to justify to the N.K.V.D. first that he had "diverted" such a large sum, and secondly, that he had let himself be robbed of it? The money was the property of the Kolkhoze! He got out of his difficulty by becoming an outlaw himself. He even asked us to make him a member of our band, but we turned him down. We were honest bandits.

Another time we heard that the payroll for a N.K.V.D. division was being transported in a horse-drawn cart over a road in our neighborhood. We held up the cart and took the money while the driver was roaring with laughter. This was our most popular feat. People were delighted at the idea that a whole N.K.V.D. had been robbed.

Every time we brought off one of our robberies, I went to visit Spanish refugees and distributed some food and money among them, mainly for the children. I told no one where I had got it from, and nobody asked. Once a transport of Spanish children were about to be sent to Ufa by road. Badly clothed and starved as they were, the danger that many of them would not survive the journey was very great. When we shared out the booty after one of our excursions, my fellow bandits gave me an extra 240,000 rubles to buy food and clothes for those children. In spite of all this, I put by enough money to finance my expeditions to the frontier. But when I came back at the end of August, my hoard was exhausted. I devoted the month of September to banditry again. By then I had earned a new nickname. Among the outlaws of Uzbekistan I was called "The Spaniard." They used the title respectfully. As a bandit, I was a success.

AT THE BEGINNING of October I heard that several foreign armies were being formed in the region of Moscow, destined for the coming campaigns in Yugoslavia, Bulgaria, Hungary, Czechoslovakia, Poland, and the Baltic States. Foreigners were permitted to join as private soldiers, even if their nationality was not that of the particular country of destination. At once I decided to try to enlist. To be sent abroad with such a unit might give me my chance of escape. But first I had to get back to Moscow.

My wife was there already. Her parents had been so shocked by the frightful conditions at Kokand that they had arranged for her to go to Tiflis; from there she returned to Moscow with her mother, as soon as the danger to the capital had passed.

I had no identity documents which would serve for this journey. My legal papers fixed my residence in Kokand. The forged papers I had used on my trips to the frontier would not have stood up to the frequent controls of all travelers on the way to Moscow. Also, I intended to volunteer under my own name, properly identified. In the end I risked going to Moscow with my legal papers such as they were.

Although I was arrested three times in the course of my journey, I never came near a police station. Each time I was able to bribe the police agents. I slipped through most of the control points by a simple but effective trick. When the agents asked for my papers, I would produce them from my wallet, but at the same time fumble with some photographs as if I meant to hide them. Invariably the agents pounced on those photos, which were taken during the Spanish War and showed me in uniform. Then they could not help discovering that I had been a Spanish Army commander and at once became respectful. It was even better when they recognized El Campesino. Then they treated me as a revolutionary hero whom it would be dangerous to offend. The Russians had publicized my coming to the Soviet Union, but kept my fall from grace very quiet. The few times when my identification did not finish the matter at once, I produced a packet of cigarettes and half a bottle of vodka, and that gave me all the prestige I needed. On the whole, I found it not too difficult to get to Moscow.

Moscow was a very different city from the one I had left in 1941. Authority and an iron discipline had been restored by ruthless terror. With victory in the air, the government had no need to appeal to the people. It was more totalitarian than ever. In 1941 the officers of the Soviet Army had been humble and afraid of the people, afraid of being made responsible for the setbacks. Now in 1944 they behaved as if they wanted to wipe out that humiliation. They were arrogant and cocksure.

In the factories the normal working day was twelve to fourteen hours. In many cases the workers of one shift were kept on for the next as well. This helped the technical staff to establish records and earn kudos at the expense of the famished, exhausted workers. Even school children had been drafted into factories and Kolkhozes, and did little less work than the grownups. Everywhere in the streets were long queues in front of the shops, and people did not dare to grumble. The shops themselves were full of American goods with Russian labels. Privileged members of Soviet society were able to buy them at special rates and resell them on the black market. Vodka was no longer on ration, but its price was fabulous. This made me very sorry to have gone back to the capital!

I reported for work at the underground. The fact that I turned up so suddenly caused no surprise and brought me no trouble. After all, I had not been dismissed from my job, but simply evacuated from Moscow like most other people when it looked as if it would be taken by the enemy. I did not dare, however, to live with my wife. The check kept by the N.K.V.D. was too close. At the first inspection they would have seen from my papers that I was in Moscow without a permit, which would have meant three years' imprisonment, and that I had been ordered to forced residence in Kokand, which would have made it far worse.

To seek refuge with friends would have been wrong and senseless. Anyone courageous enough to let me stay in his home for a night risked deportation on being found out; and the police kept a sharp eye on people's visitors. For a man without a lawful abode there was only one way of staying in Moscow in relative safety, to find a different tart each night and let her take him to her room. Prostitution is illegal in the Soviet Union. But the street markets of Moscow were full of prostitutes, though not all of them were professionals. To those women whose whole existence was outside the law it did not make any difference if they had dealings with somebody who also lived outside the law. In an emergency they would give a part of their earnings to the N.K.V.D. militiamen who caught them out—naturally the real professionals were well known to the N.K.V.D. guards. And then there was always the lure of tobacco and vodka, which the guardians of the law could not resist.

For a month I slept every night in a different room, in the company of a different woman.

This was a surprisingly long time to keep out of the clutches of the N.K.V.D. I succeeded, oddly enough, because my mates at work were convicts. Before my evacuation, the people with whom I worked were mostly Communists in disfavor and, so to speak, on probation, like myself. Therefore we were watched and spied upon the whole time. After my return to the underground, my gang consisted entirely of men who had been sentenced to hard labor. This meant that the N.K.V.D. knew all there was to know about them. The first control at my place of work came after a month. But when it came, it naturally led to the discovery that I was in Moscow without a permit. I was arrested, and faced the certain prospect of at least three years in prison.

I would have disappeared from sight without further ado, if one of my mates had not managed to inform my wife. She set to work at once, through her powerful friends, and was successful up to a point; I was neither tried nor sentenced. But her influence was not strong enough to secure my release. I was to be deported to Kazakstan, where at that time German prisoners of war and Germans from the Volga Republic were being concentrated. They did not allow me to say good-by to my wife, who was pregnant. With no other clothes than those in which I had been arrested, they put me on a train. Two agents escorted me. They agreed with me that an endless train journey without vodka and tobacco would be a terrible bore. At the fourth station from Moscow they let me get out of the train to buy the necessary. I was quick to disappear among the crowd in the nearby market. Next day I was back in Moscow.

But this time I had no papers at all. They were in the pockets of my escort. Most likely this had been the reason why the agents let me out of their sight so easily. A Russian policeman feels that he holds a prisoner almost as securely when he has taken away his papers as when he has handcuffed him.

In truth my situation was desperate. I decided to call on the committee of the Spanish Communist Party, together with my wife, though I might have known I had nothing to hope for from those people. At the office I found the Valencian Communist Uribe and the Colonels Cordón and Galán Jr. Uribe was in charge of the Spanish Communist refugees in the U.S.S.R.; Cordón and Galán were studying at the General Staff College. When the three saw me there, they were greatly surprised. One of them said, "Well, well, we thought that they had hanged you by now!" "Or that you were a lifer," said another.

It was not exactly a friendly welcome they gave me. Even so, I should have known better than to answer as I did. But I was never strong on tact. I retorted, "It's you who ought to be in jail, cowards that you are, leaving your comrades in the lurch! And especially the children...."

We were at once in the middle of a violent quarrel. I accused them of having fled to Ufa, together with government and Comintern leaders, without a thought for the Spanish refugees for whom they were responsible. I shouted that they had thought only of their own miserable skins, of keeping their soft jobs as hangers-on of the Kremlin and the Comintern; that they had come back to Moscow after deserting their comrades to play at being the big bosses, and so on. They answered back. We were all shouting at each other at the same time, with every insult and good Spanish oath we could think of. The noise was so great that it alarmed people in the next room. The door opened and in rushed La Pasionaria and Lister. They joined in the row at once. Out of their own mouths I heard that it was they who had prevented my release which my wife had nearly managed to obtain, and they who had arranged for my deportation to Kazakstan. They boasted that they could do what they liked with the lives of Spanish refugees, with the help of the N.K.V.D., and threatened me with the full use of their power. I shouted, "One day the Spanish people will call you to account for all your crimes, in Spain and here!"

"Maybe," La Pasionaria answered angrily, "but you won't be alive to accuse us."

"Let's go," said my wife. She was in tears. "You won't get anything out of these tigers."

La Pasionaria turned to her and threatened, "You'll pay dear for helping this Trotskyite dog!"

We left. The violence of the dispute had terrified my

wife. She feared that La Pasionaria and her followers would make things even worse for me, so she tried to mobilize her most influential friends. First she appealed to Stalin's daughter, an old friend of hers; nothing came of it. Then she turned to the secretary of Kalinin, Gorki, who had been one of the witnesses at our marriage. Gorki persuaded Kalinin to see me.

Ariadna and I arrived at Kalinin's office at three in the afternoon. She came along as my interpreter, as she sometimes did, for my Russian was not good enough for a complete mutual understanding.

President Kalinin received me in a fatherly manner and said, "I can see how difficult it is for you to adapt yourself to Soviet discipline. You are still too much the Spanish individualist. This time I can get you out of trouble, but I won't be able to protect you indefinitely. I'm afraid you will finish in Siberia if you go on taking the bit between your teeth."

He gave orders to issue temporary identity papers to me. As he saw how badly I was dressed, he even gave me some money for new clothes. Kalinin often made gifts of this kind to people who sought his help in other matters. Then he invited me to come again and tell him how I was getting on.

I did go after some time, to show him the new suit I had bought with his money and to thank him for his understanding sympathy. This time he received me rather coldly. He had had a report from the Spanish Committee which painted me in deepest black. But I still remember him with gratitude. It is perhaps the only grateful memory of this kind which I retain from my ten years in the Soviet Union.

XI

WITH THE PAPERS provided by Kalinin, I could at long last tackle the project which had brought me to Moscow. In June, 1944, I made my first attempt to enlist in one of the foreign armies in formation. I chose the Polish Army. But it was more complicated than I had imagined. To be accepted, even as a private soldier, a volunteer had to prove that he had never been convicted of a crime and that he was otherwise reliable. I met the first of these two conditions; in spite of the many disciplinary measures I had brought upon myself, I had never been formally convicted. It was different with the second condition. Of all the foreign groups, the Poles were the most exacting in their standards of reliability. They decided that I was not a sufficiently reliable character. They were right. I had no intention of being reliable.

The next group I tried were the Yugoslavs. Their army was being formed at Kolomna, about eighty miles from Moscow. An officer I knew from Spain took me into their camp. But there I became suspect as a spy, was arrested, taken before the commanding officers, and threatened with being shot on the spot.

The reason why I had aroused suspicion was that I had declared myself to be El Campesino. The Yugoslavs saw at once that this must be a lie—why should one of the famous generals of the Spanish War try to join a foreign army as a private soldier? The story sounded too thin. They had no idea who I was, but were certain I could not be El Campesino. If I used his name, it must be for a special and dangerous purpose. Hence I could only be a spy.

The reasoning was unanswerable. I might well have been shot there and then, if I had not had a stroke of luck. A colonel whom I had met during the Spanish War turned up and vouched for my identity. He told me, "You may give thanks to the Lord or the devil that you've come across me. In Spain you were a good Communist commander. I wouldn't like you to get shot."

On his intervention I was set free, but he refused to help me to join the Yugoslav Army. He realized that I was in disgrace with the Russians and was afraid of compromising himself with me.

I did not try any other army unit. Feeling trapped and frustrated, I hit upon the idea of appealing to the one person in the Soviet Union who was able to cut any Gordian knot. At the beginning of August, I wrote a letter to Stalin.

As far as I remember, it said: "It seems unworthy to me that, at a time when the Russian people shed their blood in a life-or-death struggle against Nazism, a man like myself who has proved his mettle in the Spanish War should go idle in the streets of Moscow. If there is proof that I am a counterrevolutionary, let me be executed without consideration. If not, I ought to be employed in the fight or else allowed to go abroad."

I am not sure that Stalin ever saw my letter. But I did get an answer. Two days after I had handed in the letter, two colonels of the general staff came to see me. They assured me they had come on behalf of Stalin himself, and subjected me to an endless, detailed interrogation. First they took notes of the story of my whole life— Soviet officials are crazy about biographies! Then they wanted to know my precise opinions on a number of political and military problems. I took the cross-examination with bad grace. It was a battle between us.

The battle lasted six days. Early each morning they took me in their car to general staff headquarters, to the secret department of the N.K.V.D. where Beria himself came to work at times. There they would resume their interrogation and carry it on till late in the night, usually one o'clock in the morning. Fifteen or sixteen hours of interrogation! Their tactics varied. Sometimes they would speak to me as kind friends, offer me one cigarette after another, and give me paternal advice. At other times they would be brutal, put me through a ruthless search, and threaten and insult me. They wanted to wear me down. It was I who wore them down.

They finally told me that I would hear the decision on my case through the Comintern and the Spanish Committee. It was clear that they wanted to evade responsibility and were afraid of passing judgment on a well-known foreign Communist. At a later stage it might be decided that they had made a mistake about me, and then they would have to pay dearly. What it all amounted to was that I was being delivered back into the hands of my personal enemies in the Spanish Committee. I knew they would not, and could not, permit me to enroll in a unit destined for service abroad, and still less let me leave the U.S.S.R. on my own. To wait for their verdict meant to wait for my arrest and deportation to Siberia. I saw that I would have to make my escape from Soviet Russia now.

Under certain conditions it is easier for several people than for one alone to organize an escape. In my opinion this was the case with my flight. I needed assistants. It was easy enough to find others who wanted to get out of Russia. After all, nearly all the Spanish refugees, most other foreigners, and not a few among the ruling class were dreaming of it. It was quite another matter to find companions I could trust with my plans and their execution. I decided on two young Spaniards, Lorente and

Campillo, who were devoted to me. Shortly before the end of the Civil War, in which they had served as pilots, they had been sent to the U.S.S.R. for special training. At first they had been treated very well; later they had fallen in disgrace and passed through great hardships. Now they made a living as best they could; Polish friends let them have shoes and clothes which they sold on the black market. But they did not like this form of existence. Also, they went in constant fear of arrest.

I knew the two as bold, resourceful, and determined men. They respected and feared me. We agreed to attempt the escape together. But I imposed severe conditions on them: They had to obey me blindly; disobedience was punishable by death; once we had started they had to go on with me in all circumstances; they had no right to ask any question about details of my plans; if one of them were to fall into the hands of the N.K.V.D. he had to let himself be cut to pieces rather than sell or betray the others. They accepted my terms.

Above all we needed money, a large amount of money.

In Kokand I had become used to taking the money I needed from whoever had it. It never seemed robbery to me to take from thieves what they had stolen, and only thieves had ready money then. Now I again knew somebody who was in possession of stolen wealth, and felt no scruples about taking it from him. He was a Polish Jew who had been a lieutenant in the International Brigades in Spain. When I left Moscow in 1941 I let him have the use of my room. After my return I had been there several times. I had seen that he had plenty of blankets, suits, and shoes, all rarities in Russia, and that he also had a great deal of cash. The origin of his wealth was no secret to me; he had held an important job at the International Red Aid for three years.

I went to his room together with Lorente and Campillo. We took 50,000 rubles and as much of his marketable things as we could carry, while he was cowering in a corner. I threatened to kill him if he denounced us, but I might as well have spared my breath. He could not denounce us, because then he would have to explain to the N.K.V.D. how much he had stolen from funds which belonged to unfortunate people in need of aid. This was a graver crime than robbing an individual. If he had reported our theft, he would have been in greater danger than we.

Once we had the money, I applied for an appointment with Marshal Zhukov. While he was my instructor at the Frunze Academy he had always shown a liking for me. Now he received me in his enormous room at general staff headquarters, with great cordiality. I had come to see him accompanied by Lorente and Campillo. After a few minutes of general talk I drew him aside, onto a balcony, under the pretext that I did not want my companions to overhear us. Then I explained about my wish to be sent to the battle front as a simple volunteer. Zhukov began to laugh and said, "What? The famous Spanish general, my old pupil, fight as a private soldier? Surely there's something better for you in the Soviet Union!" He promised to take my case in hand and asked me to come to see him again in a few days' time.

So there I was, with the possibility of going back to a position of privilege in the Soviet regime. With Zhukov's backing I might still have had a career in front of me. But I decided to do nothing about it. The idea of climbing back to power at the price of the misery of the common people, like the other profiteers of the regime, did not please me. And then, although I had not yet lost my faith in the Communist idea, I had lost all faith in the Russian sort of communism, or what is called communism there. I had made up my mind not to stay under the control of the Kremlin, whether as one of the exploiters or one of the exploited. Finally, I was bound to Lorente and Campillo. They had sworn not to turn back once we had started on our project. I could not turn back either and leave them in the lurch.

In any case, my private talk with Zhukov had been nothing but a blind. While I was holding his attention and keeping him away from his desk, Lorente and Campillo had carried out the mission which was the real purpose of our visit. They had pocketed some sheets of paper with the letterhead of the Soviet general staff and a rubber stamp with its seal. This gave us what we needed to fabricate our own marching orders, apparently issued by the highest military authorities in the U.S.S.R.

That very night Lorente and Campillo went on another delicate and difficult assignment which netted us the rest of the necessary equipment. The two handsome young men had courted and won the favor of the young wives of two N.K.V.D. lieutenants. In the evening they took them to supper and gave them plenty of champagne. Afterwards, in the ladies' homes, they plied them with brandy until the women lost interest in anything that happened around them. Lorente and Campillo took away a careful selection from the wardrobe of the two absent husbands. In the meantime, I obtained other indispensable items from a general who was not only a very kindhearted man but also the best friend the Spaniards had in Russia—he dreamed of going back to the Spain he loved. The next morning the three of us boarded the train to Baku: a short, broad, swarthy lieutenant of the N.K.V.D. counterespionage service, and two younger lieutenants of the partisan corps, in whom nobody suspected El Campesino, Lorente and Campillo.

Our journey was uneventful. The papers we had manufactured were unimpeachable; our bad Russian astonished no one, because there were many others like us in the special services. On August 18, 1944, we were in Baku. Our next problem was the special permit, issued on the spot, for the crossing of the Caspian Sea to Krasnovodsk. We got it thanks to the combination of our uniforms and papers with a generous tip to a N.K.V.D. lieutenant in the port of Baku. But then we had to wait two days for the next boat to sail, and we also had to buy the tickets. Both involved the risk of being asked about the purpose of our stay in Baku and our crossing to Krasnovodsk. Fortunately we were able to pick up three grass widows whose officer husbands were at the front and who were so pleased with our wining and dining that they put us up at their homes. The ladies even bought our boat tickets for us so that we were kept out of the public eye. We reached Krasnovodsk on August 21, and left it two days later in the train to Samarkand.

Now we were on the route which I had so carefully investigated a year before and for which I had laid my plans. In a small handbag I carried a chess set, three bottles of vodka, and a large supply of excellent cigarettes. Without delay I made friends with the chief conductor of the train and invited him, as a brother officer, to a game of chess. When he saw me opening my bag and taking out not only the chess set, but also bottles, he accepted eagerly. Then, while he and I were immersed in our game, Lorente and Campillo fed him with drinks and cigarettes. From time to time, N.K.V.D. agents carried through their usual strict check of travelers in this frontier region. Then our new friend would tell them, as soon as they entered our compartment, "Can't you let us go on with our game in peace? These fellows are all right, don't you see?" And he would point to the bottles. The N.K.V.D. men were anyhow inclined to accept on trust any officer wearing the uniform of their corps, but the assurance of the official who had full executive powers on the train and with whom they had to deal every day settled the matter. On their tours of inspection, the agents stopped with us only to have a drink. They never even asked to see our papers.

In the small hours of the morning the chief conductor was so drunk that I persuaded him to go to his compartment and sleep it out. By that time the other passengers were asleep and the visits of the N.K.V.D. agents had stopped. Towards four in the morning the train began to slow down for what I knew to be a small, out-of-the-way station. At this moment I told my companions that we would get off the train here. They stared at me in bewilderment. Campillo said, "But we aren't even half way to Samarkand!" "We aren't going to Samarkand," I answered. That was all. Without a further word, they made ready. I told them to leave most of our luggage behind so that it would look as if we meant to come back. Slowly, unhurriedly, in the most natural manner we could summon, we got out at the rear-end of our coach. It was an exciting moment. As far as we knew, nobody saw us go. Once outside we plunged into the darkness and began to walk very quickly, but in complete silence. At a safe distance, we stopped and took civilian clothes from the suitcase we had brought along. When we had changed into them, we put the uniforms into the suitcase and hid it away among the shrubs. Then I took the lead on our march through the dark.

My comrades found it trying to follow me without a question about my plans, as they had undertaken. Campillo asked, "Where are we?" I answered sharply, "We're going to the Persian frontier. It's a long way and a hard way. Buck up now, and don't ask any more questions. And if we meet any frontier guard and suchlike, we've got to kill him—without making any noise, if that's possible." I had a revolver which a Spanish friend had got for me on the black market in Moscow, but I was determined not to use it if it could be avoided. The sound of a shot might be fatal.

Lorente and Campillo had no choice but to be content with my brief explanation. The way ahead was quite as long and hard as I had told them. The mountain region we were in was difficult to cross even by the few roads and footpaths, but these we dared not take. We followed an almost straight line, away from any beaten tracks. Luckily I had a good compass; also, I was trained, ever since my boyhood, to find my bearings by the sun, the moon and the stars. In daytime we went into hiding. Two of us would sleep, the third take a turn at keeping watch.

During the day the N.K.V.D. patrols kept to heights from which they could see any suspicious movement down in the valleys; at night, they came down into the valleys and patrolled particularly the points where roads and paths crossed. Therefore we had to do our walking by night and keep to the most difficult route, up in the mountains.

I was an old mountaineer, schooled in the wild hill ranges of Estremadura, but in this savage, hostile country I needed every bit of skill I possessed. We cut ourselves stout and tall sticks which we used to test the ground before us in the darkness. The sticks also helped us to pull each other up on very steep slopes and to support each other on narrow ledges.

We carried as much food and water on our backs as we could manage, and I rationed it strictly. All the same, our supplies were exhausted at the end of the fourth day. By then we felt hungry after our strenuous nightly efforts and on our small rations, but we had to go on with no other food than edible plants or roots. We were not particular, but the region was barren and we found very little. After the fifth night, our stomachs began to ache with emptiness. What fretted us most was thirst. There was little water, and wherever it was to be found, small groups of tribesmen had settled down. Those groups had every interest in being on good terms with the dreaded N.K.V.D., more so in a frontier region. It would not have been safe to let them see us. It would not have been safe to let anyone see us in a district where everybody was forced to be a N.K.V.D. informer, because to see a stranger and fail to report it meant severe punishment. We had to approach the smallest spring with the utmost caution. Sometimes it happened that we came within sight of water only to see that people were near it. Then we had to creep away, our throats burning with thirst, and to do it as cautiously and noiselessly as we had crept near. It was much harder then.

The first to flag was Campillo. He was afraid that we would die in the mountains before reaching the frontier. Contrary to our pact he wanted to give up. But we could not have left him behind. He might have been caught, and then Lorente and I would have been in immediate danger. There was no time for half measures. I told him bluntly that he could either come on with us, or get killed by me on the spot. He came on with us.

At three in the morning on August 30 I suddenly gave a shout and stopped. Lorente and Campillo stopped too. "What is it?" asked Lorente. I pointed to the freshly plowed ground in front of us. "A plowed field—so what?" he said.

I answered, "It's not a plowed field, it's the frontier."

From my excursions I knew that the frontier hereabouts was marked by a strip of plowed land, several yards wide.

Campillo rushed forward, but I caught him by the

arm and pulled him back. "Don't step on it," I said. For I also knew that the Soviet border patrols had no qualms about crossing the frontier in search of fugitives. The fear Russia inspired in Persia was so great that the N.K.V.D. were not only the real masters of the border country on either side of the frontier line, but also of a large area of the other state. If we had walked across this freshly plowed strip of land, our tracks would have betrayed us. So far we had not seen a single frontier guard and to the best of our knowledge nobody was looking for us, nobody was aware that we were in the region. But tracks leading across the telltale strip would have warned the guards that someone had made his escape, and they would search for us.

I sat down at the edge of the sweet-smelling clods and took off my shoes and socks. My companions followed my example. Then, carrying our things in our hands, we walked across the turned-up soil—*backwards.*

If they discovered our tracks now, they would take them for those of barefooted peasants and not think it worth their while to chase after us. Or, if they did try to find out who had crossed the frontier, they would first look on the wrong side. And we would gain time.

As I was moving backwards, I felt how the soft, crumbling earth under my soles gave way to hard, unyielding ground.

I was in Persia.

XII

HOW CAN I describe what I felt when I stood on Persian soil and looked across that strip of plowed land to the country I thought I had left forever? For a moment I was filled with exultation. Then the joy was gone, blotted out by the sorrow and bitterness of shattered hopes. The country I had left behind was the same in which I had once believed. I had thought it to be the home of human freedom; now I saw it as freedom's grave.

And my comrades, the friends with whom I had fought for the victory of Communism—what would they think of me? They would call me a deserter, traitor and counter-revolutionary.

Once there was my wife; there would soon be my child. Had I condemned them to Siberia through my action?

I had achieved my aim. I had escaped. But it was without gladness that I led my companions away from the frontier, into the interior of Persia.

    ✻   ✻   ✻   ✻   ✻

At dawn we reached a small village. The villagers met us with suspicion. They were not used to anything good

[121]

coming to them from the other side of the frontier. But when they saw our ragged clothes and our state of exhaustion, they soon lost their fears. We cannot have looked like Soviet agents to them. They gave us food and drink. Then they spread out their prayer rugs, prostrated themselves, and said their prayers. It was as if they were praying for us.

Rarely have I met people so simple and good. It was comforting to find a warm human concern for the suffering of others after so much cold disregard. Neither our Russian, nor that of the few villagers who spoke it at all, was very good, but we made ourselves understood to each other. It appeared that they hated the Russians because they would cross the border, steal sheep, cows, horses, and corn from the poor peasants, and carry off those who resisted or protested too much. I tried to tell them that we were Spaniards, but they had never heard of Spain, so I said we were from Spanish Morocco. This meant something to them. Men from North Africa almost belonged to their race. They grew even friendlier.

We learned that the nearest railway station was between two and three hundred miles away, or so we computed it. The villagers explained how long it would take us to get there by tracing a great curve with their arms to indicate the course of the sun, and repeating it for the number of days. They also made it clear that this part of their country was infested by Russians, so that we still would have to avoid the roads, move cross-country, and hide from sight unless we wanted to be dragged back to the Soviet Union.

At this news Lorente and Campillo lost heart. After our brief spell of ease among those friendly people, after the moment's illusion that our difficulties were over, it was hard to face more days and nights of crawling through the shrub like hunted beasts.

Lorente had at least an adventurous spirit. At the outbreak of the Spanish War, when he was no more than a boy, he had stolen his father's hunting rifle and run away to fight against Franco. Campillo was no older—both were in their mid-twenties—but he lacked Lorente's youthful boldness. When he realized that our hardships and dangers were to go on he rebelled openly. Neither of them was wanting in courage, but the last few days had been too heavy for them. I had imposed an iron discipline and forced them to long marches with little time for rest. I doubt whether we would have reached the frontier otherwise, as we could hardly have lasted another day without food. But the two young men were in no condition to see this. Again I had to use the final threat to make them go on: They could continue the journey with me, alive, or stay behind, dead. This had been our understanding when we set out, and I held them to it.

With as much food as we could carry, the gift of our Persian friends, we resumed our march. This second journey was a repetition of the first, only it lasted longer. In addition we were now plagued by lice. With our single razor we shaved off the hair on our bodies, but even so we continued to be devoured by vermin. It was not only physically irritating, it was also demoralizing.

Then our provisions gave out. Lorente and Campillo felt the hunger more than I did, because they were younger. It made them less cautious about going into villages in search of food. Sometimes, when a settlement looked large enough to be of interest to the N.K.V.D., I strictly forbade them to take the risk. If we did enter a hamlet it was only after the most careful scouting, and this exasperated them. I had to hold them back time after time. Sometimes I deliberately insulted Campillo to rouse his self-respect and spirit. On the eighth day we took shelter in a copse. While Lorente and I went to sleep, it was Campillo's turn to keep watch. When I awoke, he was gone. We had to leave the spot immediately, tired though we were. If Campillo fell into Russian hands, he might give us away and even lead them straight to our resting place. It was an unfair suspicion, as we found out later, but we could take no chances.

On the tenth night we reached the railway line and shortly afterwards the small station to which the peasants had directed us. The station master became our guardian angel. He told us that N.K.V.D. agents were posted at all the larger stations and checked traveler's papers. A few local trains were less closely watched; by taking one of those we might escape attention and investigation. But it was three days before the next train of this type would come through. What to do in the meantime? The station master solved our problem for us. He was an educated man, spoke Russian, and hated the Russians bitterly, not only as a Persian patriot but also because several encounters with the N.K.V.D. had given him a taste of their methods. He took us to a place where we could safely hide, not far from the station and his home, brought us some clothing, and gave us four whole packets of cigarettes. At nine in the morning three days later, he put us on the train he had selected, recommending us to a Persian police officer, a friend of his, who traveled on it. When we said good-by to him he mumbled, "You'll need some money," and pushed ten *tumens* into my hand. Then he backed away with an embarrassed smile. In our position, it meant a small fortune. He is a man I shall always remember with deep gratitude.

It was eleven that night when we left our train at Teheran. Nobody had asked for our papers during the journey, nobody asked us for them when we went out of the station together with the crowd. After Russia where one might be asked for one's identity papers a dozen times a day, it seemed incredible that anyone should be able to come off a train in the capital of a country and freely walk out into its streets without being asked a single question about his person and business there. Incredible? To me, it seemed anarchy.

My reaction after our arrival at Teheran shows to what extent a human being may become used to the loss of his individual liberty. With all my rebellious spirit, five years in the U.S.S.R. had so accustomed me to an existence under strict official control, restriction and direction, that my first response to the sights of Teheran was indignation. A city where the market overflowed with goods, where everybody bought and sold what he liked, where people went to the theater as they pleased, and read the newspapers they fancied—what a muddle, what selfishness, what anarchy!

Lorente, who had never been an ardent Communist, saw things differently. Bitingly I said to him, "As soon as you're outside Soviet Russia, you begin to feel like a Fascist!"

As I see it now, this remark showed that I had not thrown off the influence of Stalinism, in spite of my disillusionment and flight. I still spoke like a good Stalinist to whom everything disagreeing with Soviet doctrine is "Fascist." I had escaped from the country; I had not escaped from their propaganda. In the end I was to discover that I had not even escaped the country for good, and that it was the last remnants of Stalinist thinking in me which led to my undoing.

Five days we wandered through the streets of Teheran in freedom. We did not go to a hotel. Even in Persia one cannot stay in a hotel without having the right sort of papers. In any case we had no money except what the station master had given us, and no prospect of getting more for some time; we could not afford a room at a hotel. But Teheran is full of cheap doss houses where people sleep on the floor and are not asked for papers. There we spent our nights. We spent our days walking through the bazaars which were always crowded, day and night, always noisy, always full of color and light.

There were other things we did, apart from sampling the street life of Teheran. I was looking for ways and means of getting back to Europe. It had come to my ears that some officers or delegates of a small Polish Army which was being organized in North Africa were in Teheran on a recruiting mission. I thought they might enlist Lorente and me. From North Africa we would be able to get into Spain and organize guerrillas against Franco.

Lorente and I called at the legation of the Polish Government in London. The consul treated us with great courtesy and asked us to come back the following day. Unfortunately we did. We were met by four men armed with tommy guns. We had been taken for Russian spies. The Poles hustled us into a car and delivered us triumphantly to the British Military Mission.

The British were more intelligent and more considerate than the Poles. They were quick to realize that we were genuine refugees from the Soviet Union. But—they did not let us go.

It was not a disagreeable form of detention. They gave us good clothes and excellent shoes, and fed us like princes. We got a fresh set of underclothes every two days, and our sheets were changed every week. Our rooms were cleaned by two colored servants. We were well supplied with wine, beer, and tobacco. I have had some experience of captivity. This one was the pleasantest I can remember. But captivity it was.

The British officers who came to see us were invariably courteous, friendly, and pleasant. One of them, a captain, spoke Spanish and Italian. With characteristic reserve he told me only after several visits that he had fought in the Spanish War as a volunteer. He proposed that I should let them send me to England, and assured me that I would not be asked to work for the intelligence service. My counterproposal was that they should send me to North Africa, from where I meant to re-enter Spain. He told me that he could not do that for me. It was at this point that the remnants of my Stalinism proved disastrous. If I had been clever, I would have accepted the British offer, whatever my ultimate intentions. In this way I would have put myself out of Russian reach, and nearer to Spain. Yet I had imbibed the Communist vocabulary for so many years that England was a synonym

[128]

for "imperialism" to me. To go there, under the protection of the British, and obviously because they wanted to make use of me in some way, seemed a betrayal. Therefore I refused.

Perhaps I missed a great opportunity. Would it have been impossible for me to return to Spain once I was in Europe? Was not the moment when Mussolini and Hitler fell from power the right time to overthrow their henchman, Franco? Would it not have been feasible to build on the ruins of Franco's dictatorship a genuinely Spanish Communism, independent of Moscow? Nothing of all this occurred to me at the time. I was still caught in the snare of the Communist slogans about Britain and British imperialism. And so I missed the chance to be on the spot when Franco was most vulnerable. I missed a chance to alter the course of history.

My mental blindness of that period did not prevent me from seeing the kindliness of those British officers. I know they did what they could for us, within the limits of discretion. I repaid them in the worst and most foolish fashion. Lorente and I had been British prisoners from October, 1944, to January, 1945, when we decided to make our escape. The time of our daily walk in the prison yard was the best opportunity. At about five in the afternoon three Iranian soldiers would take us to the large courtyard which was separated by a wall from the Teheran Hospital. Some 160 yards from the spot where we took our exercise, walking up and down, there was a postern in the wall. Our guards were armed with rifles and long knives, but boredom made them inattentive. One afternoon when it was getting dark we suddenly made a dash for the little door. Our guards came running after us, shouting, and brandishing their knives. Luckily for us they made no use of their rifles. Two of them caught up with us just at the postern; the third ran out of the yard, probably to get help. The soldier who came to grips with me slashed me twice with his knife, once across four fingers of my right hand, once across my head. I knocked him out and turned to Lorente, in time to see him drop. The second soldier committed the mistake of helping his comrade instead of attacking me. I slung Lorente across my back, broke through the door, and was swallowed by the dusk in a matter of seconds. Lorente had been stabbed near the groin and it was some hours before he was able to walk, but we got away because the hospital was on the outskirts of the town where the settlements ceased.

We got away, but our mad flight meant that not only the Russians, but also the Persians and the British were after us. Unfortunately it was the Russians who caught us.

* * * * *

We were slowly plodding through the snow, under a cloudless sky. My eyes began to ache from the dazzling sunshine. First I squinted, then I closed my lids to a mere slit, then I covered my eyes with my hands to protect them. It was too late. I had to give up and admit that I could no longer see more than a glimmer—snow blindness! Now Lorente had to lead me. We were heading south, towards the Persian Gulf, but so far we had not got farther from Teheran than eighty miles. My idea was to find a railway line running in the right direction and ride in a goods train. Both Lorente and I had done it successfully in Russia, and we thought it would work in Persia as well. But Lorente was less experienced at steering true course than I was; after some time he confessed to having lost his way. He told me that a small village was in sight, but we doubted whether it would be safe to approach it. At this moment we heard the noise of an engine running nearby with a stuttering beat. "Wait here, I'll see what it is," said Lorente. I waited, shielding my eyes with my hand until he returned.

Apparently the engine we had heard was that of a mill which belonged to an Armenian. The man spoke Russian, and Lorente thought he could be trusted. He led me to the mill. The Armenian received us cordially and eased my snow blindness by washing my eyes with tea. Then he gave us something to eat. All the while the engine was stuttering and stopping and running again. The Armenian asked us whether we knew anything about machinery and would be able to repair the motor which operated his mill. We thought we could do it. Lorente was a good mechanic, trained on airplane engines.

"If you can make it run smoothly, I give you fifty *tumens,*" said our host. Fifty *tumens* would be wealth to us. Lorente dismantled the engine and I helped as soon as my eyes permitted; in the end we had it purring in perfect rhythm. The Armenian was delighted. He let us stay with him for several days and even took us hunting. Of course we never told him who we were or that we were fugitives from Soviet Russia. When we felt rested and ready to walk on, we asked for the fifty *tumens* he had promised us. He said, "I don't have so much cash here, I'll have to go to Teheran for it." When he had left, I told Lorente that I didn't like the look of it and thought we should get away at once. "Without waiting for the money?" he asked. "If it is money he's gone for. . . ." I answered. But Lorente believed that I was unjust to the man who had been so kind to us, and I let him persaude me—worse luck!

The next morning we heard cars driving up from several directions. Our Armenian was back, and with him a squad of N.K.V.D. men with tommy guns. They had come on three roads simultaneously to make sure that we could not escape them.

It was an excellent business deal for the kind Armenian. His engine was repaired. He had saved fifty *tumens* and probably earned a reward. Above all, he had won the good will of the all-powerful N.K.V.D.

At first we attempted to deny that we had come from Soviet Russia, and insisted that we were residents in Persia looking for work. The Armenian however pointed out that we spoke Russian but not a word of Persian. The Russians considered their case as proved. They put us into a car and took us back to Teheran, directly to the Soviet consulate. At no stage did we have a chance of appealing to the Persian authorities. Thus our experience taught us to what degree Russian influence was dominant in this part of Persia then; Russian agents were free to make arrests on foreign territory. I have been told that the N.K.V.D. detained nearly 200,000 Persians and took them away to labor camps in the Soviet Union. Persia had so little real independence that her own citizens could not be sure of protection by the laws of their country. What might a foreigner expect, then?

At the consulate we were put into a cell and our interrogation began. I had been careful not to reveal my real name, but the young woman who was called in as an interpreter had worked in Spain during the Civil War and recognized me at once as El Campesino. My denials were useless; she would not be shaken. I became a "special case," was separated from Lorente, and taken at night, under elaborate precautions, to a lockup about fourteen miles from Teheran.

On the way there I had an attack of violent despair. I wanted to force my escort to kill me. In the car I began to shout and struggle with all my strength. But it is not easy to choose death at will once one is in the power of the N.K.V.D. They muffled my head in a greatcoat and choked my cries, almost choking me—but not quite.

My new cell was a dark and damp hole underground. From there I was taken to interrogation. The clothing and shoes I had been given by the British were evidence in the eyes of the N.K.V.D. officers that I had sold myself to the British espionage service. As I protested that this was precisely what I had refused to do, and that my sole wish had been to get into Spain and fight against Franco, they beat me unconscious. When I came to my senses, I was back in my dark cell. There I lost track of the time, but I believe it was five or six days before I was moved to another N.K.V.D. center in Persia, again at night, handcuffed and in foot irons. Again I was questioned and beaten senseless; this time the ordeal lasted eight or nine days. Finally five N.K.V.D. men armed with tommy guns escorted me back into the Soviet Union— back into the great prison from which I had escaped. The bitterness I had felt on crossing the frontier into Persia was nothing compared with what I felt when I was taken across the frontier into the U.S.S.R.

They drove with me to Baku and wanted to leave me in prison there. When the Baku prison authorities refused

to accept me, my guards were compelled to take me farther on to Tiflis, the regional headquarters of the counterespionage service. The first thing the Tiflis police did was
to take away my English suit and shoes, not forgetting
socks and handkerchiefs, and give me instead the shabby
uniform of a soldier in the Red Army. Then they left me
in my cell for five whole days, alone and without food.
At the end of those five days the door of my cell opened
and in came a man who addressed me by name in a pleasant and friendly tone. He introduced himself as Captain
Nikitin, the "procurator" or examining judge. I learned
from him that Campillo had indeed been captured after
he had left us, had passed through the Tiflis prison, and
was now in the Lubianka prison in Moscow. Though he
had been tortured, his statements were favorable to myself and Lorente. Lorente was in a cell near mine. From
him and Campillo Captain Nikitin knew the detailed
circumstances of our flight. Both had corroborated what I
had claimed from the beginning and consistently, that
our only aim had been to return to Spain and take up the
underground struggle against Franco. At Nikitin's advice and request I signed a statement to this effect.

Nikitin made it plain that Lorente and I were about to
be transferred to the Lubianka prison, and that our interrogation and trial for espionage would follow. He did not
hide from me that I would probably be tortured. But
he was unfailingly friendly and considerate, gave me

tobacco, and saw to it that I had enough to eat. My ten or twelve days in Tiflis prison were an exception—the only one of its kind among my prison experiences in Russia, just as Captain Nikitin was the only exception among the hyenas who administer so-called justice in the U.S.S.R. I shall always be grateful to him—or to his memory, for men like Nikitin do not last long in such a post.

When I was put on a prison train bound for Moscow, I had recovered some of my strength. I needed it at once. Our coach, nicknamed the "thirty-year-car," was reserved for men convicted of espionage, which meant a sentence for life even when the formal sentence only specified fifteen, twenty, or twenty-five years' hard labor. The compartment into which I was pushed had room for four passengers. There were sixteen of us. When the door slammed, we found ourselves pressed into a single block of flesh. And once the train had started, the door was not opened again for four and a half days.

So we were ferried across Russia, a solid mass of starved, thirsty, half-suffocated creatures who became something less than human. Not being able to move, we were racked by terrible cramps. We slept standing, and satisfied our necessities standing. With every hour the atmosphere in this foul box grew more pestilential. As the train rattled on, we drifted into a state of blurred semi-consciousness in which the brain ceased to think and the senses to feel.

At Rostov the door was opened. We had a breath of air, a drink of water, and a little food. First I drank, for the ordeal by thirst had been worse than the ordeal by hunger. Then I turned to the food. Each of us was given three hundred grams of black bread—scarcely eleven ounces—and a few sprats. I tasted the sprats; they were so salty that I forced myself not to eat them. I had heard stories about prisoners on long transports like ours, who had gone mad or died of thirst from eating those salt fish, before being locked up again. We could not know when we would taste water again. I did not risk the sprats and ate only the bread.

Then the door was shut on us again and the train moved on. Our taste of air, food, and water had revived us and we felt the horrors of the journey more acutely, until we sank back into merciful insensibility. After five more days we were unloaded in Moscow.

When we pried ourselves loose from one another and shuffled out of our box, two bodies fell to the floor. Two men were dead and must have been dead for some time. They had died on their feet, held up by our packed living bodies, and nobody had noticed it. The smell of death was not stronger than the general stench, and their immobility not strange where no one could move. In the midst of fellow sufferers, they had died in fearful loneliness.

XIII

AFTER THE PRISON train came the prison van. It was a huge windowless car with a central passage flanked by eight or nine cubicles on each side. A guard thrust me roughly into one of those cells. My face was glued to the outer wall of the van, the door pressed against my back. In this fashion I was brought to the Lubianka prison, on one of the first days of March, 1945.

To begin with I was put into a *sobatchnik*—a "kennel." It was a closet with just enough room either to stand or to sit on a stool with one's knees touching the door. After two hours I was taken for a medical examination which, in reality, was a ruthless and thorough search of my body. It was carried out by a woman with the red star of a N.K.V.D. captain on her white overall. To the best of my belief, a woman was employed for those intricate manipulations to make the humiliation worse for the men. She handled me brusquely, with utter callousness. After she had turned back my eyelids, they went on hurting for four days. To probe my ears, she used a sort of wire which left them bleeding. I cannot bring myself to describe the way in which she exploited my anus and urethra. Then she examined my mouth and esophagus with a tube carrying a minute light bulb on its end. During this procedure I vomited four times—as intended. At the beginning of the examination I had to swallow a piece of bread and a quart of foamy water which tasted of soap. The idea was to make me throw up whatever I might have tried to hide by swallowing it.

When the torment was over I felt sick, full of loathing, and unspeakably humiliated. To prolong the humiliation, which was one of the main weapons at the Lubianka, I was not given back my clothes but taken to my "kennel" completely naked. I spent the night naked, a March night in Moscow! The next morning they gave me a pair of short trousers, ending at my knees, and a shirt with only one sleeve. My jailers were good psychologists. They realized that tragedy may inspire strength and a sense of one's own worth, therefore suffering had to be turned into something ridiculous. It is difficult to decide whether I found my nakedness—the absence of the customary shelter of clothing—more demoralizing, or that clown's outfit which made it impossible to face anyone without a shaming sense of being a figure of fun.

They left me in the "kennel" for six days, with nothing to do except to wait—for what?—and to recover from standing by sitting, from sitting by standing. A guard outside the door kept constant watch on me through the Judas window, as though to tell me: While you are here, you cannot make a single gesture or movement without being seen by us. This was the first lesson of the Lubianka.

Next I was put into a cell which had already five inmates. They were so pale, weak, and emaciated that I thought it was a sick cell and that these men suffered from grave diseases. Under cover of the noise which the guard made in locking the door, one of the five—later I knew him as a Lithuanian—whispered to me, "You'll stay here for a year unless you die before." I retorted, "I don't die so easily!" The five looked at me with astonishment and pity. They must have thought: He is new here, he doesn't know yet. I believe I was put in the company of those wretched, half-dead men so that I should see what the future would make of me.

Our cell was approximately fifteen by eight feet large. Three bunks were ranged on each side along the longer walls. They were too short for a normal man to stretch out, and we had to sleep with our legs doubled up. The lower part of the walls was painted a dirty, sickly green, the upper part a gaudy ochre. Each of the colors was unpleasant by itself. Together they were maddening for somebody who had to see them day after day, week after week. It was a comparatively small thing—what does it matter if walls are ugly—but it was one of the details of

the prison regime which were designed to attack the
senses of the most insensitive prisoners.

Our muscles were mortified by the impossibility of
stretching out when we slept and by the rigid positions
we had to maintain during the day—I shall have to say
more about them in a moment. Our sense of sight was
tormented by the staring ugliness of our surroundings.
But our sense of hearing was subjected to torture by silence. The walls were so thick that each cell was insu-
lated. We were forbidden to speak to one another in the
cell, and a microphone made it possible for the guard
outside our door to hear the slightest whisper. This rule
was particularly hard to bear. Communion and comradeship, the means to relieve our discomfort and break the
monotony, were within our reach, but we had to resist
the most human urge, the urge to speak, because it was
forbidden to us.

Our day began at five in the morning. Then we had to
get up from our cramping bunks and were allowed seven
minutes to go to the toilet. There was one toilet, and the
six of us had to use it in turn within the seven minutes. It
was our one and only opportunity during the whole day.
In the cell we tried to control the demands of our body,
but it was rare that all six were able to contain themselves
for twenty-four hours.

During our seven minutes' absence, the guards made
a careful search of our cell. After our return, we had two

hours to clean it out. We had to wipe our bunks with a rag soaked in paraffin, and polish the floor with brushes. If the guard discovered that we had left the smallest spot, we were put to work for another two hours. It could have given us some relief from doing nothing, but exhausted and weak as we were, it was punishment.

When we had finished the cleaning, we got our breakfast, three and a half ounces of black bread and a mugful of warm water. And then followed a different kind of torture. We would have liked to lie down on our uncomfortable bunks for a rest after our labors. The rule however was that we had to sit on them in an upright position, our legs and knees close together, a book in our hands, never for a moment allowing ourselves to relax or slump. Each had a book in his hands and longed to read, but the regulation demanded that he keep his eyes fixed on the peephole in the door. If one of us forgot himself and sought escape in his book, the door would open almost immediately and the guard would call him to order with blows.

At one o'clock we were given our midday meal. It was an almost unbelievable ritual. A man dressed as a waiter, in blouse and tall cap of glistening white, brought on a silver-plated tray under silver-plated dish covers, for each of us another three and a half ounces of black bread and a hot soup made of tomato and sour cabbage. To have this miserable food served to miserable men in miserable surroundings by a neat, elegant waiter, was a master stroke of refined cruelty, another touch of that buffoonery which was destroying our spirit as much as our abject suffering itself.

Between half past one and two we were allowed—or rather, ordered—to lie on our bunks. From two to seven we again had to sit in rigid postures, our eyes fixed on the peephole. Our evening ration came at seven and was a repetition of our midday meal. Then another hour and a half sitting on the edge of our bunks, staring at the peephole. And then at nine, to bed. To bed but not to rest. It was not part of the program that some of the prisoners' strength should be restored during the night.

I have already mentioned the cramped position to which the shortness of our bunks forced us, but this was not all by any means. Prison rules obliged us to keep our arms stretched out on top of the blanket, however cold it was, and keep them so that the guard could see them all the time. In addition, our faces had to be turned towards the door even during our sleep—if we managed to sleep—so that the first thing our eyes saw on opening was that relentless spyhole.

If a guard noticed that a prisoner had changed his position in his sleep he would burst into the cell and buffet him awake. The guard had no difficulty in keeping a check on us because the bright electric light was kept burning the whole night, stabbing through our closed lids into our brains even in our sleep. But, sleep? It was no real sleep. We piled the fatigue of the night on the fatigue of the day and woke more tired than we had gone to bed.

❖   ❖   ❖   ❖   ❖

Which feature of this prison regime contributed most to the physical and mental disintegration of the inmates of the Lubianka?

The hunger was bad enough. A prisoner of the Lubianka could not have died of starvation, even had he wished for it; skillful, systematic underfeeding would merely turn him into a brute stupefied by lack of food. His whole body would ache with craving for plenty of food, enough to eat his fill for once, and for different food, anything but the eternal black bread and cabbage soup.

Sleeplessness was worse. As we got up, more exhausted than the night before, we would feel stupor creeping over us. We would feel our eyes sinking deeper into our skull and our skin sticking to our bones, and a hollowness within, as if all life had been sucked out of us.

Worst of all was our obsession with the eye. When we kept our eyes glued to the peephole, as the prison rule imposed, we saw behind it the eye of the guard, unceasingly fixed on us. We could never escape from its watchful glance. Did we really see the eye? It appeared so, because the guard would quickly come into the cell to punish us if we ever looked away. And yet, I ask myself whether it could have been physically possible that there was no moment in which there was no eye at the Judas window. The strain would have been almost as bad for the guard as for us. Possibly the guard was relieved at frequent intervals. Possibly a painted eye was sometimes stuck up on the other side of the door. We could not have gone close enough to make sure without bringing harsh punishment down on us. In any case we did not argue or think it out lucidly while we were there. It did not matter. The main thing was that we thought the eye was there and believed that we saw it.

We saw it day and night, awake and asleep. All our nightmares centered round the peephole and the eye. When we were sitting motionless on our bunks, tortured by the almost irresistible temptation to move, the hole filled by the eye at which we had to stare seemed to grow until it covered our whole range of vision. At times it would seem to rotate, faster and faster, dragging our confused thoughts into a whirl of nothingness.

The Lithuanian suffered more than the rest of us from this spell. His eyes would bulge and follow an imaginary circular movement of the peephole. Then he would begin to drool at the mouth and to move his head in small circles. Usually it was only a moment before the guard burst in, rained blows on his unresisting body and pushed him back into the prescribed position. But soon

[145]

afterwards the Lithuanian's head would start moving again as if by itself, always in the same circle, while his eyes were fastened upon the peephole and the eye.

A human being was disintegrating.

Once a week came an interruption. A doctor with the rank of a major would enter our cell, accompanied by a couple of N.K.V.D. officers. With the greatest amiability he would interrogate each prisoner about the state of his health, and ask whether he had complaints about the food or wished to write to his family. If a new prisoner was foolish enough to accept this offer, his letter would be passed on to the examining judge in charge of his case.

Nevertheless this weekly visit was more than an elaborate mockery. In combination with the reports of the guards, the reports of the medical inspector recorded the reactions of the prisoners, assessed their stage of physical and mental weakness, and made it possible to decide when they were ripe for questioning.

The regime to which we were subjected was nothing but a preparation.

XIV

THE MEDICAL INSPECTOR considered that I was in the right frame of mind for cross-examination when I had been in the Lubianka for one month.

Night and darkness have always been the allies of inquisitors. It was always at night that I was questioned—every night for two months, and nearly every night for another six months.

One day I went to bed at nine o'clock, according to rule. Twenty or thirty minutes later, when I had drifted into sleep, two guards pulled me out of my bunk and gave me two minutes to dress. Then each grasped one of my arms and so I was marched out of my cell.

The corridors of the Lubianka are endless. I was taken through a long passage, into an elevator and out again, through another long passage, into and out of another elevator, through a third long passage. I do not believe that it was really such a long way to the interrogation rooms. Probably they prolonged the journey to impress me with the vastness of the prison, or to give me more time to suffer from apprehension, or both.

[147]

The corridors of the Lubianka are silent. Thick carpets deaden the sound of steps. The prisoner is led to his doom along empty, silent passages. On the rare occasions that another pair of guards in charge of another prisoner appear at the end of a passage, the first ones click their tongues, as one does to a mule or dog, swing their prisoner round, and keep him with his face pressed against the wall until the second party has passed. A prisoner of the Lubianka must never see any fellow prisoners except his cellmates, not even when he is transported in the prison van. If his own friends are in the cells to the right and left of him, he is not told. He must feel completely alone.

When my guards arrived with me at the entrance to the interrogation rooms, I had to sign a register. The woman behind the desk held a shield over the page, with a slit just wide enough to sign one's name on the blank space. It was impossible to see the signatures of other prisoners. When my guards delivered me to the examining judge, he signed a receipt for me. On leaving after interrogation, I had to sign the register again. In the Lubianka they are meticulous about their records.

I was brought into Room 967, a large, severe, well-lit room. The walls were bare except for the obligatory portrait of Stalin facing the door. One N.K.V.D. officer in uniform sat at a table, two others were standing near him. I was told to sit down in a corner, eight yards from them, and to put my hands on a stout wooden board in front of me. I was in a pen. And then I waited. Nothing happened. The officers said not a word and pretended to read their newspapers, but their eyes were on me all the time. I was so tired that I could hardly keep awake. After more than an hour they suddenly started firing questions at me, as if they had silently agreed that the waiting had worked sufficiently on my nerves. They had distributed their roles. The officer who had been sitting when I came into the room spoke in a patronizing, friendly, and affable tone, while the other two insulted me in the foulest language. But I knew the matchless Russian vocabulary of abuse and blasphemy well enough myself, and from my corner I paid them back in kind.

The questions came so quickly that I scarcely had time to answer. When had I begun to work for the British and North American imperialists? Hadn't it been during the Spanish Civil War? The N.K.V.D. had kept me under observation for many years. For instance, they knew I had been in touch with a certain American officer attached to the U.S. Embassy in Madrid. How often had I seen him? What secrets had I passed on to him? How much had he paid me?

I answered with jeers. The weekly inspectors had been rash when they reported me ripe for questioning; I believe my behavior disconcerted my inquisitors. Their game was clear from the beginning. They meant to pass a harsh sentence on me, but they also wanted to destroy my whole past and dishonor me in the eyes of the world and particularly of the Spanish Communists. El Campesino had been a cheap agent of the Anglo-American imperialists already in Spain. Why had I led thousands to their death? To weaken the Republican Army! Why had I committed countless reprehensible acts? To discredit the Communist cause! And why had I wanted to do all that? Because I was a paid lackey of the Anglo-Americans, of course! No wonder the British at Teheran had received me with open arms and provided me with good clothes and money—I had earned it in their service. Those clothes were here as conclusive evidence against me.

I answered, "Certainly not. When the English saw what rags I was in after living in the Soviet Union for some years, they gave me clothes. I needed them badly. Now you've stolen them from me. That's all there is to it."

My first interrogation ended at four in the morning. It was not continuous. From time to time they stopped and seemed to forget my presence. Then, after a long pause, they pounced on me again to catch me off my guard.

The whole game was repeated all over again the following night, all the following nights. I was rudely wakened after my first half hour's sleep and sent back to my cell in the small hours of the morning. The questions, the intervals of silence, and the roles played by my interroga-

tors followed the same pattern. There were a few varia-
tions though. It became obvious that they checked
answers I had given the day before, and that they based
some of their questions on additional information which
could come only from one group of people, the Spanish
Committee in Moscow—my old comrades, who were
hounding me down, working through the N.K.V.D. One
point, however, was not brought up as an accusation
against me though they had it on record and that was my
banditry in Kokand. The N.K.V.D. did not bother about
that.

On the fourth or fifth night, the three officers filled one
of the intervals by passing round photographs and making loud comments, just as if I had not been there. The
comments were meant for me. They told me clearly that
those were photographs of my wife, Ariadna, and of my
newly born baby daughter. It was in this form, in Room
967 of the Lubianka prison, that I first learned I had a
daughter. When I begged them to let me see the photos,
they refused, but continued their mocking remarks. The
child wasn't like me at all. Was I sure I was the father?
Of course, my anti-Communist activities had kept me
away from Ariadna so often and so long that a better
Communist might have taken my place with her. This
was right and proper. She needed another man now when
I was lost to her for good. But what should they do with
her? Leave her free so she could divorce me and marry

the other man, or arrest her as my accomplice? They found my affection for my wife a good weapon against me.

At the end of each session, I was ordered to sign a statement which recorded questions and answers, and each time they told me to confess the crimes of which they accused me. I never signed anything. After two months they concluded that stronger measures were called for. I was not taken back to my cell but put into the "kennel."

I answered with a hunger strike. They let me starve eight days, perhaps expecting me to break down, and on the ninth they put me into a strait jacket. They pulled the straps so tight that I could hardly breathe and fed me a liquid through a tube. Retching and choking, I had to swallow it. After an interruption I resumed my hunger strike. Again they put me into the strait jacket and fed me soup through a tube. I saw that I could not win in the unequal battle and gave up my attempt. They went on with the interrogation.

Altogether they questioned me during eight months. On most nights they did not let me sleep more than two hours and a half, often not more than an hour and a half. I thought no longer of food but only of sleep. Sleep is the worst of all obsessions. In daytime it cost me a super-human effort not to provoke the blows of the guards who came into my cell as soon as I began to doze. At night, it took me another supreme effort to stay awake during the interrogations, especially when the examining judges did not speak to me for hours on end, and to meet the quick fire of their questions. In the end I answered without thinking at all, by sheer instinct and out of crude obstinacy.

The only thing that counted was the crying need of my body for sleep. They shouted questions, the insults, the blows meant nothing. I craved sleep. I thought of nothing but sleep. And yet, each time they thrust a prepared statement before me and asked me to sign it, I refused without a thought. Anything might have been said in those statements—I wouldn't have known. I was incapable of reading and understanding. But I never signed. I never confessed anything.

At last my interrogators decided to apply the final means of persuasion. When I had once again refused to sign a statement, they called in my guards, and one of the officers gave the order, "Take him to the freezing bath."

On the floor below, in front of a small door, my guards ordered me to undress. Then, with practiced skill, one of them pulled the door open, the other pushed me through it, and slammed it shut again.

Powerful jets of ice-cold water struck me from everywhere. They came from the walls, the ceiling and possibly—my memory is confused—from the floor. The sudden impact of that icy shower which comes without the slightest preparation, without a transition, and strikes the naked, defenseless body at every point is such that the muscles are at once paralyzed, the heart refuses to function, and unconsciousness follows in the wake of an anguish similar to a grave heart attack.

After some moments I lost consciousness. I woke up in the "kennel," still naked, dripping, and shivering. It was hours before my frozen body ceased to shake.

Although the immediate pain of the freezing bath lasts no more than a few moments, the shock it causes is so great that it is the most dreaded torture of the Lubianka. Most prisoners who have been through it once collapse when they are threatened with it again. I passed through it not once but several times. For even after the freezing bath I refused to sign a confession. I was sent there again, and still I refused to sign anything.

How did I hold out where it would have been normal and human to break down? I do not know. I think that the hard life I had always led made me exceptionally tough. Also, in my case the interrogators were defeated by their own tactics. By depriving me of sleep for such a long time they turned me into an unreasoning brute who acted from the obscure dictates of instinct. But before I reached this stage, and while I was still capable of thought, I had fixed my mind stubbornly on not signing anything. Later, when I could only act by blind instinct, that mental command had become a part of instinct

[154]

itself. I was incapable of changing my mind, for it functioned no longer.

Of all the prisoners subjected to the regime and methods of the Lubianka, probably not more than one in a thousand has resisted to the bitter end, and even fewer among the Russians. The Soviet inquisitors know their own people well, particularly their Party members. Foreigners puzzle them. They had not counted with the fact that I was not a Russian, with all that capacity for renunciation and submission, with that lack of individual pride and self-esteem, which seem inbred in them. Yet as a rule they succeed even with foreigners. Their first questionings are designed to probe the prisoner's weak spots, to experiment with the kinds of attack to which he is most susceptible, and to test his powers of resistance. Then they use their accumulated knowledge for the real attack. There comes a moment when the prisoner feels he is caught like a fly in a spider's web, his vital substance being sucked away until he is nothing but an empty shell. By then he is usually ready to purchase relief—a little more food, a little more sleep—by agreeing to sign at least some part of the confession which is demanded of him. He believes that this is just a sop to the judge, something that does not matter. But it is only the beginning. Now the inquisitors have discovered how to make him yield, and they press on to make him yield further. How can he withdraw what he admitted the day before?

Unless he has the unexpected strength to retract, the signed statement of yesterday leads logically, inexorably, to the wider statement he will be asked to sign today. With the first concession he was lost. In the end he confesses everything, only to be left in peace. If this means death, what of it? The sooner it comes, the better.

There was a period when such confessions meant death for the Soviet prisoners, but under Beria the system was different. For a time capital punishment was abolished by law, though it was reintroduced later. In any case the regime now found it wasteful to kill its prisoners quickly and mercifully. Instead they had first to give their last ounce of strength in the mines, timber forests, and workshops of Siberia until hardship and overwork killed them. Soviet economy reaped great profit from the agony of its victims. This was the final achievement of the most perfect machine ever devised to disintegrate and dehumanize human beings. Its first achievement was the complete dehumanization of the judges, officials, and police who work it.

I am one of the few who defeated that machine. But I defeated it only in so far as I did not let it wrest from me a signature or confession which would have acknowledged its justice. In another sense it could not be defeated. The refusal to confess led neither to acquittal nor to release from the clutches of the N.K.V.D. My stubborn resistance did only one thing for me: It sent me to my fate with the knowledge that I had not bowed down before those unjust judges.

The end came without preparation. Towards the end of my ninth month in the Lubianka, I was escorted from my cell to the prison van. Once more I was pushed into a cubicle, my face to the wall, the door pressing into my back. If others were in cells next to me, I did not know it. As the van started with a jolt and I was rocking back and forth in my dark closet, I knew that my long battle with the inquisition was over, since I was here, but nothing more. Nobody had told me anything. The prison van carried me towards the unknown.

* * * * *

My first destination turned out to be the prison camp of Butyrka.

On my arrival I was thrust into a cell full of naked men. Why they were naked became immediately understandable. In a room measuring some 450 square feet, 180 to 190 prisoners were herded together. The air was foul and thick, the heat stifling. Nearly everyone had taken off his clothes because they were unbearable in this oven. I soon found that the few exceptions to this rule were the weakest prisoners, those who did not dare to take off their clothes because they would not be able to defend their property against their thieving cellmates. I also found that the most dangerous thieves, and the masters of the collective cell, were common criminals.

This was my first acquaintance with a prison hierarchy I was to meet in other camps as well. At the top were the guards, then came the common criminals—murderers, thieves and cutthroats—who lorded it over the others, and lowest were the political prisoners.

Most of the guards at Butyrka, and in a good many other prisons and labor camps as well, came from Kazakstan. They were young men, between twenty and twenty-four, rather short in build but extremely strong and tough, with large heads of Mongolian cast, and small, cunning eyes glittering with cupidity. After the four years for which they had enlisted, they would be posted to Kolkhozes in their native country. In the meantime they had absolute power over us, might beat us or kill us, or rape the women, and be certain they would not be called to account. They exercised these privileges mainly against the political prisoners. We were the "counter-revolutionaries," the "fascists," for whom no treatment was bad enough. Only to the ordinary criminals did the guards show a certain respect. They found it easy to make common cause with them because they belonged to the same breed. And then, the criminals shared their loot from the "politicals" with the guards, to whom politics meant nothing and enjoyment of their term of power everything.

In our cell, a score of common criminals terrorized the rest of the prisoners. From the start I showed them that I did not accept their dictatorship. I began by fighting for, and winning, a place on the floor to stretch out. (We had to sleep on the ground, without any cover, but this meant no special hardship in the sweltering heat of our crowded cell.) Next I made sure of my few possessions by announcing that I would kill anyone who dared touch them. The leader of the criminal gang got the impression that I was a prominent bandit, and hastened to assure me of his friendship. After this his group did not bother me.

On my third day at Butyrka I was called to see a N.K.V.D. major—he came in civilian clothes—who greeted me politely and gave me tobacco and food. This was a change indeed after the freezing bath! The reason for it became clear when he advised me to sign the prepared statement he had brought with him. Such an act of co-operation, he explained, would be taken as a sign of my good will and make it possible to review my whole case in a different light. When I failed to co-operate, he became rather less friendly and read me the sentence that had been passed against me: three years of hard labor at Vorkuta Camp, in the polar region of Siberia; five years of forced residence, and five years of loss of all civic rights; altogether thirteen years in the hands of the N.K.V.D., which might well become a life sentence.

Most prisoners who arrived at Butyrka began to serve

their sentence before they even knew that it had been passed and what it contained. But a prison camp had advantages. It was not a sealed tomb like the Lubianka. The time of investigation and interrogation was over, and prisoners were allowed to write to their families. Of course this did not mean that they could write real letters. They could merely fill in the blank space of printed forms, to let their families know that they were alive and ask them to send food and tobacco. When parcels arrived, they were stolen, of course, by the criminals or the guards. Often food parcels would continue to come long after the prisoner had been transferred to his final place of destination, a fact of which his family was never informed, and the only ones to benefit from them were the guards.

I was supposed to be on hard labor from the moment my sentence had been read to me, even while I was in temporary camps. I had registered as a builder because of my work at the Moscow underground. Therefore they made me a sort of foreman at Butyrka. My task was to organize the working gangs of men and women. Every night at ten, two guards took me through all collective cells, and I had to pick out up to eight hundred people fit for work on the following day. It was then that I came to knew the horrors of the female prisoners' existence.

The women were kept in five large collective cells, crowded together like the men, and like the men they went more or less naked. Most of them were no longer young, and they were dirty, unkempt, gaunt, and repulsively ugly. But there were some young girls too, fourteen, thirteen or even twelve years old—what "enemies" to the regime! The most depraved among the elder women made vicious use of them.

While I put names on my list and selected workers for the next day from this pitiful herd of human cattle, the guards would take their pick of the most attractive young girls. One or two guards at least dragged their victims into the passage outside. But more often a guard would fling the girl to the ground and violate her then and there, with the others looking on. If she struggled or screamed, some of the other women would hold her down, shut her mouth with their hands, and then the assault would take its course amid shrieks, laughter, and obscene jokes. I had never imagined anything like it and thought nothing could be worse, but I found that the night of the general monthly bath was infinitely more horrible. The orgy there revolted me so much that I could not bear to go on making my list and threw paper and pencil on the floor. At once the guards jumped on me and beat me senseless. I came to myself in the infirmary. As a rule they take no notice of routine beatings there, so I must have had an exceptionally large dose.

The insatiable sexual appetite of the guards caused the worst incident during my time at Butyrka.

A young peasant girl had been put into a collective cell. As a newcomer, she was not forewarned or hardened by experience, and when a guard wanted to rape her, she put up a desperate fight. Her shrieks were so heart-rending that some of the male prisoners in the next cell began to beat with their fists on the wall. Most of those men were common criminals and not particularly squeam-ish, but they were also young and had not had time to become quite so cynical as their elders.

When the noise from the men's cell grew louder, a hush fell on the women. They knew the price to pay for "collective protests." The men too knew it, and demon-strations of this sort were very rare. But there are times when it is impossible to keep oneself under control, and this was one of them. Only a few men had started beat-ing against the wall, but the contagion spread and a wave of madness drove the whole crowd in the cell to frenzy. They battered against door and walls, shouts and insults swelled the noise, and the whole prison shook.

The guards ran in a body to the rioting cell, with their tommy guns. They pulled the door open and fired one round, and another, and a third. Then the barking of the guns stopped, and the prison was quiet, but for the groans of the wounded and dying.

The wounded were carried to the infirmary, the dead were buried, and the guards were praised by the administration of the prison for their prompt action in stifling a "mutiny."

* * * * *

From Butyrka I was sent to the camp of Krasniya-Presnya, a relay station on the way to Siberia. The commanders of the various labor camps sent guards to Krasniya-Presnya to fetch the prisoners destined to work under them. They were known as "the slave traders." I spent four months in Butyrka and Krasniya-Presnya waiting for the slave traders to come for me. It was in January, 1946, that they finally delivered me at the Siberian labor camp to which I had been sentenced—to which I had been condemned.

XV

UNDER THE NAME of Komisaro Piotr Antonovich, with papers which mentioned neither my past nor my real identity, I arrived at the town of Vorkuta on a day when the thermometer showed eighty-five degrees below the freezing point. The N.K.V.D. officer who decided on the prisoners' places of work saw immediately that I was in better physical condition than most, and suggested that I should become a Stakhanovite. He said, "If your output and your conduct are satisfactory, I'll see that you get good papers at the end of your term. If not, you know what to expect: a dog's life and a dog's death."

I intended to survive, and therefore I had to win the confidence of the officials. And by now I knew how to do that. I answered the officer that I was a loyal Communist in spite of my sentence, I would try hard to be one of the best Stakhanovites and do my share to convert the arctic desert into the richest region of the Socialist fatherland. He was delighted. I was assigned to a coal mine and sent to the corresponding labor camp. There I reported to the camp commander. When he heard my bad Russian, he inquired about my nationality. I said I was Spanish, but did not offer further explanation. The commander was greatly interested. He said that his assistant had been in the Spanish War, and sent for him at once. When this assistant, a lieutenant, saw me, he exclaimed in surprise and threw his arms round me. He had been aide to General Lukacs whom I had known well—a famous Hungarian general of the International Brigades who was killed at the front, just in time to escape disgrace and arrest by the Russian secret service in Spain. Naturally the lieutenant explained to his chief who I really was. He did it in the most favorable terms. This was a good start for me. But it did not change the hard facts of my situation. I still remained subject to the same cruel regime as my fellow prisoners, and to the same murderous climate, which at first I thought I would not be able to stand.

Vorkuta means "people of the underworld." The first human beings who settled in those frozen "taigas" north of the Arctic Circle were deported prisoners. Now there is a town of Vorkuta, the administrative center of the Vorkuta region and of its camps which supply labor for the mines, the new factories, and the land. The Soviet authorities plan to turn the Vorkuta into one of the most productive and densely populated areas of the U.S.S.R., and this they can achieve only through slave labor. North of the timber forests is the great arctic plain where the soil thaws only for a brief spell in summer, and then only on the surface. Underneath the crust is the solid depth of everlastingly icebound earth. In July and August the climate is bearable, but soon the ground freezes again. And when the polar night begins, the Vorkuta is a black, icy hell. Only the doomed prisoners work on, night or day, ice or thaw.

In the Siberian winter it is impossible to be out of doors unless one is completely covered. The least carelessness means frostbitten limbs and amputation. A man alone would not be able to stay alive in the open when the fierce storms sweep the tundra. One has either to cling to guiding ropes or join hands with others in a chain. The watchdogs of our guards sensed the approach of a snow storm before we did; they began to howl and whine, and this would be the signal to start cutting holes into the frozen ground where there was no other shelter. If a storm lasted for many hours—and some lasted for days—men crouching in such holes were buried under the snow and froze to death.

One day it happened that 150 prisoners, a shift on its way back to camp, were caught in a sudden storm only a few hundred yards from the mine. The guards abandoned them and made their way back to shelter with the help of their dogs. The prisoners dug themselves in. Two days later, when the storm abated, the next shift going to the mine passed small white mounds. Nobody troubled to dig the bodies out. But one of the officers in the camp command said, "It is a pity we've lost their clothing."

With the possible exception of the two summer months, a successful escape through that vast wilderness was virtually impossible. Yet the measures taken to guard us were strict and elaborate. The Vorkuta camps had three, and in some cases four, barbed wire fences. Elsewhere they had these fences, or stockades, or stonework topped by barbed wire. In our camps, the three fences were set up at a yard's distance from each other. The first and second were connected by an electric cable through which a strong current could be sent in an emergency. Between the second and the third fence roamed the watchdogs. There were at least four of them, and in the biggest camps eight; they were not tied up but kept each to its beat by barriers. The dogs were the spoiled darlings of the camp administration, trained to obey the guards and hate the prisoners, and better fed than the N.K.V.D. men themselves. If a prisoner did succeed in getting away, the dogs were let loose. There were cases where they not only killed but mangled and devoured escaped prisoners. But in any case, whether the dogs killed a prisoner or not, the punishment for attempted escape was death.

Every camp had at least four watch towers, one at each corner. They were manned by one guard during the day, by two at night. These sentries were armed with revolvers and tommy guns. Powerful searchlights were mounted on each tower. To simplify precautions, the whole camp had a single entrance gate.

Within a camp there were twenty to twenty-five huts for the prisoners, 130 by 30 feet in size. Usually they were built of wood, sometimes of a sort of felting. Two rows of planks along the walls and one row in the middle served as beds: bare planks, no blankets, no straw. Of course we slept fully dressed. If our clothes were wet, they had to dry on us—or not.

Each hut was occupied by 150 to 160 prisoners. For sanitation we had buckets which were emptied in the morning and sent out their foul stench throughout the night. For heating we had a single stove in the middle of the hut. The punishment huts or *vouros* had no heating at all.

No camp was without its *vouro,* an unheated shack with small cells, twelve foot square, where prisoners were locked up for the night, completely naked. The only way not to fall asleep and freeze to death in the cold seasons was to keep moving, to jump and run, and beat one's body with one's fists. I was among the most favored prisoners, but I had to spend several nights in the *vouro.*

In this camp we slept and lived, if one can call it living, but for our work we were taken outside under heavy guard. Each group of a hundred was escorted by six

soldiers with tommy guns. On the march, one of them
went in front of the column, one at the rear, and two on
each side, accompanied by two dogs. Any prisoner who
left his place in the file or bent down to pick up something risked being shot. The guards fired at the slightest
provocation.

Prisoners whose place of work was more than ten miles
from camp were taken there in lorries, in loads of thirty-
five guarded by one soldier with a tommy gun and a
watchdog. During the drive the prisoners had to squat
on their heels, a position which left them exhausted before they started work.

The workers' gangs consisted of thirty-five prisoners
under a foreman, a prisoner himself, who had to act as a
slave driver unless he wanted to invite punishment. At
the end of each shift a bell was rung. Then the workers
had to sit down in groups of five and were counted by a
guard, while a checker compared their output, as reported by the foreman, with the quota set to each gang.
If the target had been reached, the foreman got a voucher
which entitled him to draw the next day's rations for his
gang. If the target had not been reached, the rations
were cut by half and the foreman disciplined. Despite
this constant risk of punishment, the post of a foreman
was hotly coveted. Since he drew the rations for a whole
group, he had an opportunity to keep more than his own
share. Mostly the foremen lived on two or three men's

daily rations and so were the only ones likely to escape slow starvation.

The normal daily ration was as follows: 1½ lbs. of black bread, made of barley or oatmeal mixed with bran, sometimes even with straw, and the ingredients for a soup, consisting of less than 1 oz. of cereal (rye, barley, or coarse corn flour), 1 oz. of cabbage, ½ oz. of tomato, ⅛ oz. of oil, and a pinch of salt. These minute rations were made up into a watery soup. The black bread which was our mainstay was half-baked, the inside of the loaf raw and indigestible. Had it been baked thoroughly it would have lost three-quarters of its weight. As it was, its nutritive value corresponded to six ounces of well-baked bread. On this the prisoner had not only to live but also to work, to work like one possessed.

At meal time the prisoners waited endlessly to get their meager rations. Meanwhile they would look round with feverish, greedy eyes to see whether a scrap of food had been left somewhere. When the soup had been poured into their messtins, or any old tin they happened to have, at worst into their cloth caps, they would lap it up like pigs. There were no spoons. We did not bother to clean out our tins. Cleanliness was impossible in the Vorkuta.

Work and food, food and work, too much work and too little food; this was the vicious circle in which the prisoner was trapped. If he earned his full ration, he worked

himself into a state of exhaustion. The more he strained
himself, the more his body demanded food, more food
than it was allowed. Sooner or later the moment came,
however good his work, when undernourishment made
him too weak to fulfill his quota. Then he would be put
on the half ration, three-quarters of a pound of bread
corresponding to three ounces of normally baked bread.
On this diet he was bound to fall short of his quota again.
He was well started on the road to death.

Once a month there was a medical examination of all
prisoners. This is a misleading description, since it had
nothing to do with medical care and everything with the
drive for more work. A doctor who was an N.K.V.D.
officer, usually a woman, was in charge of the examination; three or four doctors taken from the ranks of the
prisoners acted as assistants. For the examination every
prisoner, man or woman, had to strip either in the open
or, when the cold was too severe even for us, in a room
next to the office. Then he had to wait for his turn, together with the other naked, shivering wretches. It was
a hellish sight. Our battered bodies had not even the
slight cover of their own hair or down; it all had to be
shaved off because of the vermin which infested us. We
men had our heads shaved as well. All of us were scarcely
more than skin and bones, in the literal sense of the
phrase, and the bones seemed about to burst through
their thin covering. Most pitiful and nauseating of all was

the sight of the women with their dangling breasts and protruding pubes.

Once the prisoner was before the doctors, he (or she) had to report his full name and circumstances, that is to say, the crime of which he had been convicted and the length of his sentence. Then one of the doctors would look him over and feel his buttocks. If they were still fleshy, he was listed as a prisoner fit for the highest working quota, in category I. If his buttocks were gaunt, he was listed in category II; if nothing was left but the bone and the skin, in category III. If he was so ill or worn out that he could hardly stand and do no work at all, he was no longer put into a category. Then his destination was a grim special hut. Many prisoners came away from the medical examination knowing that they had been put in a category where the work would be too much for them, knowing that they had been sentenced to death.

The doctors had no time to diagnose or treat illnesses; it would have been senseless for a prisoner to mention what was wrong with him. The task of the medical inspection was to classify the prisoners according to their capacity for work. This was all. But diseases and illnesses were rampant. Some of them were peculiar to camps of certain types. One of the worst was called the *chinga*: teeth and hair dropped out, arm and leg muscles tightened, and the victims were racked by terrible shooting pains. Some relief could be found by eating raw onion and garlic, but those were obtainable only by a fortunate few. Apparently people suffering from *chinga* did not even recover when they were sent away from the Vorkuta to a better climate. Good food could postpone death for months, but how often was good food wasted on prisoners who were doomed anyway? The *chinga* went untreated and was always fatal, as far as we could tell. It occurred in camps where undernourishment was combined with cold, and was therefore common not only in the Vorkuta but also in other Siberian camps.

Another camp disease caused a swelling of the legs; the bones seemed to dissolve to water and the victim could not keep on his feet. This disease was frequent not only in Siberia but also in the camps of Turkestan. Tuberculosis was the most common of all diseases, as was to be expected. Few prisoners escaped it altogether. Its least cruel form was "galloping consumption," because it brought quick death. Less in our northern region than in the camps of Uzbekistan, Kirghiz, Karaganda, and Alma-Ata, many prisoners suffered from heart diseases which first paralyzed and then killed them. An illness prevalent in all camps of all regions had as its symptom a constant need to urinate. Those afflicted with it had to get up fifteen or twenty times a night, and often wetted themselves in their sleep or on the march to and from work.

Women prisoners not only suffered from all these

diseases, but also from their special disorders. After a couple of years of malnutrition, many of them developed a continuous hemorrhage which caused the womb to drop. They called it the "constant drip." Young girls sent to the camp before puberty often passed straight from childhood to menopause. In some cases this led to horrible inflammations of the ovaries and to swellings which made them look as if they were pregnant.

But whatever the disease, and I have not listed all of them by any means, those of us who were able to stand, move, and make any sort of effort were classed in categories I, II, and III, and sent to the mines. Only those who were quite finished were sent to one of the special huts which existed in every camp. We called them the death huts. Nobody ever left them to return to the living world. But many of the prisoners lingered in them for two, three, or four months, waiting for the end. Their daily ration was seven ounces of bread and a pint of hot water. When they had swallowed it, they would crouch or lie on the floor, hardly breathing. Those of us who had a glimpse of them, and of their blankly staring eyes, knew that we might follow them soon.

In the Vorkuta camps, 90 per cent of the convicts had been sentenced for political offenses or "sabotage." This might mean anything. A rash word of criticism, faint praise for a foreign country, lack of respect towards a superior, may all be judged as a political offense against the Soviet system. Being five minutes late at work, taking a pencil in an office, a hammer in a workshop, a handful of grain in a Kolkhoze, making a journey without permit, may all lead to a prosecution for sabotage. Once a prosecution is started, it nearly always ends with a labor camp.

The remaining 10 per cent of prisoners in the Vorkuta camps were ordinary criminals, and their role was the same as in Butyrka. With the tacit support of the camp administration, which protected them partly from a political principle, partly out of corruption, the criminal prisoners terrorized and exploited the others. They alone showed solidarity and unity among themselves. The qualities of mutual trust and co-operation had disappeared in the other groups, but the bandits still cultivated them to carry on their banditry at the expense of their fellow prisoners. They made their own laws and imposed them so that they fitted into the rules of the jailers. They managed to smoke, to have nearly enough clothing, and nearly enough food. Theirs was the best chance of survival.

I too meant to survive. I was determined to be the exception among the political prisoners. In my favor, I had the tough constitution my tough life had given me, the rebellious spirit which had brought me to this hell and would help me to live through it, and, most important, a physical strength at the beginning of my sentence, which was superior to that of most other prisoners. I intended to use this strength to put myself in a position where I would be able to preserve it.

If I had not succeeded, I would not be telling my story. I was luckier than my two companions in my first escape from Soviet Russia. Both were sentenced to hard labor and deported to the region of Petchora. Campillo died there. Lorente managed to get back to Moscow, where he was again arrested and sent to another camp in the north. This was the last I heard of him. It is more than probable that he shared the common fate and died there. My fate was uncommon.

At Vorkuta, I started well. I promised to be a Stakhanovite, and I kept my promise. By the end of the first three months I was regarded as one of the best Stakhanovites of the region. In the coal mine I was put in charge of one of the galleries. My gang quickly rose to the rank of the most productive team in the pit.

The reasons for this success were curious and typical of the methods employed in Soviet industry. The pressure from above produces a mania for achieving record outputs—at least on paper—even if the particular record damages the level of production elsewhere in the factory or mine. Exceptionally good workers are not distributed among the others, but put in a single team. The high output of this team has propaganda value and also demonstrates the efficiency of the management. Then the exceptional achievement reached by a special team, under special conditions, is turned into a "norm" for the rest of the workers.

When the camp authorities realized that I was a foreman who might produce record outputs, they concentrated the best, strongest, and youngest workers in my gang. I organized our work as rationally as possible and fought for my team's rations as best I could. They soon learned to accept me as a comrade, which happened to few among the foremen. I was made a "workers' delegate." This strengthened my position. Newspapers in the north began to speak of "Komisaro Piotr Antonovich" as of a leading Stakhanovite who was setting an example to others.

We were working twelve to fourteen hours on a shift, without any days of rest. A prisoner had to go on working without interruption as long as the machine of his body would function somehow. There was complete equality between the sexes in this as in other matters. At first, until I got used to it, the spectacle of the women in our mine seemed particularly terrible to me. They were employed as laborers on the transport of coal and construction materials, and dragging the big, heavy sleighs in teams of three. Two women were harnessed by ropes to the front of the sleigh, like draft animals, and the third pushed from the rear. The "norm" for the women's team was the transport of nine cubic yards of coal a day.

They were in category II and drew normal rations. For all workers in category II the quota or productivity rate per head was computed at 18.4 rubles a day. Workers in category I had to reach the "Stalin quota," which was 29 per cent higher and computed at 22.4 rubles per head a day. In compensation they drew somewhat higher rations. Category III, the group of worn-out, weak prisoners who were still capable of some work, had to reach a daily quota computed at 12.6 rubles per head, on half the normal rations.

If the work of the women was hard, conditions under which the miners had to do their work underground were even harder. They seemed calculated to make it impossible to reach the targets. It happened often enough that a gang left the pit in the belief that it had done well, only to find when the figures were checked that it had failed to make the quota. The men would be sent down again, without having had their miserable meal, exhausted, and overstrained as they were. Nothing mattered but the quota, the target, the norm.

Coal mined in the Vorkuta region cost a high price in human lives. Every time I met a miner who had worked there three years, I felt astonished that he had survived at all. Accidents were everyday events. Out of five hundred colliers we had an average of eight casualties a day. The most primitive safety measures were neglected. After all, forced labor is cheap; there is an inexhaustible reservoir. The elevators in the pit shafts were designed for a load of eight persons; the guards shepherded fourteen or fifteen men into them at a time. Underground we had to grope our way through unlit galleries for nearly a quarter of a mile. Each group of five was equipped with a lamp, a lamp so begrimed and dim that we had to work in treacherous half-light. Engines were kept covered against freezing, but gases collected under their hoods and caused frequent explosions. In the dark galleries, coal trains and electric cables were a constant danger. Even the few safety rules laid down in the regulations were disregarded. For instance, one regulation for the Vorkuta mines decreed that the roof had to be properly secured by props as soon as a seam had been cut to a height of six feet. This was an important precaution, particularly in mines where the structure is such that even a six-foot gallery is likely to cave in unless it is shored up. The rule was rarely observed. Working hours used for shoring up were so many hours lost for extracting coal. Therefore the roofs were not shored up in time, as I know to my cost.

The manager of the mine where I worked was very friendly with me. He was an old Bolshevik, an ex-prisoner who had stayed at his post after serving out his sentence. I could dare to tell him my opinion of working conditions in the mine. Once he grumbled because the pit had not reached its target for several days running—we would

EL CAMPESINO

have to make up for time lost. We had been busy shoring
the gallery, and I explained this to him. He said angrily,
"But, don't you understand? I've got to have coal, coal,
and more coal. I simply can't have trouble with the camp
command." I told him that at the spot we had reached,
it was dangerous to go on working before we had put in
the props and shored the roof. "I can't help it," he answered. "You'll have to take your men back and work on
the coal, never mind what happens."

At this point the N.K.V.D. chief of the mine broke into
our conversation. He had come up behind us and suddenly asked what we were arguing about. When we had
explained, he told me peremptorily, "Do as you're told.
Your job is to get the coal. The rest is none of your business. It's time you learned that you're here to obey orders
and get the quota out of your gang." I still attempted to
argue and asked him whether they wanted bodies mixed
up with the coal. He gave me the final answer, "We want
coal. The Soviet Union needs coal. At any price." It was
unmistakable what price he meant.

We went back to work in the gallery. Some days later
I found that the percentage of coal gas there had risen to
3.75. Regulations laid down that work had to stop when
the gas rose above 3 per cent. I stopped work, led my
gang out of the gallery, and reported to the management.
But apparently the N.K.V.D. chief had made up his mind
that I was only being obstructive and should be taught a

[180]

lesson. He ordered, "Take your men back in there. And you go in first."

I did go in first and my men followed. We had hardly started work when there was a great explosion and the unshored roof came crashing down. Some of those farthest back, near the entrance, escaped unhurt. Those in the middle of the gallery had the worst of it. Ten were buried under the mass of coal and earth. I was at the innermost end of the gallery, half protected by the solid face on which I was working, and therefore I was only half buried. The N.K.V.D. chief who had intended to place me in the most dangerous spot had in fact saved my life. I was dug out by my friend, the manager, who hurried up with a team. No attempt was made to rescue the men who were completely buried.

They carried me out of the pit. I was badly injured and thought for weeks that I had a broken back. This would have been disaster, even if I recovered. As a cripple I would be useless to the masters of Vorkuta. My end would be in the death hut, and the only consolation was to think that it would come quickly. But my back was not broken. I began to mend and soon was able to hobble about. It meant a new fear, that they would put me back to work too soon. I certainly had lost something of my strength and might not be able to match my former output. If I began to fall short of my quota, I would no longer get the higher rations. Soon I might not even be able to work enough for the normal rations. And then I would begin to slide down the inexorable slope.

This was the specter which haunted me when I was called before the camp command.

The commander asked, "Would you like to be excused from hard labor for six months?" Of course I said yes. He went on, "It can be done under one condition. You'll have to serve the Soviet Union in another way if you wish to redeem yourself. I want you to tour the northern camps and speak to the deported workers. Tell them to follow your example as a Stakhanovite. My assistant will go with you as interpreter. Do you agree?"

I agreed.

The commander may have thought that I could be most useful if I recruited new Stakhanovites who would make new records and bring glory to the camp administration. I thought that the gates of Vorkuta were opening for me, for the first time, and that it was no longer impossible to think of a road to escape.

XVI

FROM THE MOMENT I had fallen into the hands of the N.K.V.D. again, I knew I would attempt to escape a second time. In the Vorkuta camp, however, it looked an infinitely more difficult proposition than the first time, and the penalty was certain death. I was ready to take the risk, because quick death was preferable to the slow death of rotting away, but I was biding my time and waiting for a reasonable opportunity. Till my accident, I had managed to keep most of my strength intact, more so than my comrades. Thanks to it I had maneuvered myself into a favorable position. Even so, I realized that I, no more than anyone else, could hope to hold out against the hardships of our existence. Sooner or later I would have exhausted my physical reserves, and then I would go down.

My injury brought it home to me that this process might be speeded up by an accident at work. I was at the mercy of circumstances. Accidents were the rule, not the exception. However excellent my record as a Stakhanovite, into which I had put so much deliberate effort, I would be written off as soon as I lost my working capacity. And yet, as it turned out, this accident was a blessing in disguise for me. It freed me from being tied to the strictly supervised route, from the camp to the mine and back. With my new permit, I was still a convict, but at least I could move outside the barbed wire. I intended to prolong this opportunity until I found the starting point for an escape which did not seem to exist for anyone trapped in the compounds of Vorkuta. The technique of handling my superiors I had now mastered—no defiance or criticism, but constant repetition of my ardent desire to prove my Communist loyalty, lip service to the regime —was going to prove its value.

Under the escort of the secretary to the camp command, my former friend of the Spanish War, I was sent on several tours to the northern camps and produced what was demanded from me, Stakhanovite propaganda speeches to my fellow prisoners. Among them I met, to my sorrow, many former members of the International Brigades who, like me, had taken refuge in Soviet Russia, and were serving sentences of fifteen to twenty years of hard labor, with scant hope of ever being allowed to leave this hell. On the other hand I became friendly with the officials in various sectors. From all those contacts I collected more and more facts and figures about the labor camps and their organization.

They were run by an oversized bureaucracy, a complicated and cumbersome machinery. A typical camp, holding 2,500 prisoners, was operated by a whole hierarchy in uniform, consisting of 6 majors, 17 captains, 66 lieutenants, 18 sergeants, 54 corporals, and 129 guards and militiamen, which worked out a rota of one jailer for every 9 prisoners. In addition, a great number of prisoners held positions of trust in clerical, sanitary and technical departments, and enjoyed small privileges for their services as spies and informers.

The commanding officer of the camp was a major, and his secretary a lieutenant. Under the camp command the following departments operated:

1) The LABOR DEPARTMENT, with a major as chief, two lieutenants as assistants, and an office staff of five. It fixed the quotas and norms for the work of all prisoners, and the rations for each category of workers, according to general directives from Moscow. The department had three subdepartments or sections: a labor section under a captain and a lieutenant, which drew up the plans for work; a medical section consisting of a major and three to five doctors who carried out the medical supervision; and finally a pharmaceutical section in the charge of a lieutenant with two assistants.

2) The LEGAL DEPARTMENT, headed by a major with two aides. The major acted as a special judge within the camp. On the grounds of the prisoners' dossiers he decided the fate of those who had served their term,

either by ordering their release or by decreeing a new sentence. A prisoner on the eve of release might suddenly find himself sentenced to a new term of hard labor, without the intervention of any judicial authority outside the camp. A records section under a captain and three lieutenants had to keep track of any offense or misdemeanor committed by prisoners and to record them in new files which then went to the judge and became the basis for new sentences.

3) The PROPAGANDA DEPARTMENT, under a captain and a lieutenant. They had to ensure the continued political "education" of the prisoners. Convicts who demonstrated their devotion to the Soviet regime by their exemplary conduct and by exceeding their norms at work were promised reductions of their sentences. The promise was not always kept. The Propaganda Department had a very powerful weapon in the personnel section which was attached to it and consisted of two lieutenants. The chief of personnel had to appoint the foremen. It meant that those coveted posts went to prisoners who had convinced the Propaganda Department of their political orthodoxy.

4) The TRANSPORT SECTION, with a transport officer who had at his disposal four chauffeurs and six teamsters, to operate two prison vans, two lorries, and six wagons.

5) The SECURITY DEPARTMENT. Its chief was a major and it had three subdepartments. The first, staffed with a captain, six lieutenants, and eighteen sergeants, had to

organize the transport and guard of prisoners on their way to and from work, and the security of the camp. The second, under a major, was responsible for the huts. The third, under a lieutenant, ran the "camp police"; this officer was in charge of thirty selected prisoners who were armed with sticks and employed a supplementary guard, and also of the cleaning squads.

6) The SUPPLIES DEPARTMENT, which made purchases for the camp stores and the kitchen, and employed a large staff, including a few privileged prisoners.

7) The PARTY SECRETARIAT, under a captain. He had a secretary ranking as lieutenant and an office manager with three helpers. This office not only represented the Communist Party, but also had the important task of making sure that the state received 50 per cent of the net value of everything produced by the camp.

The pay of all those officers, officials, and guards was combined with benefits in kind. Calculated in cash and kind together, the monthly income of majors was just over 4,000 rubles, of captains over 3,000, of lieutenants about 2,700, of sergeants nearly 1,000, of corporals nearly 800, and of ordinary guards a little over 600 rubles.

The average cost of food and clothing for prisoners was 85 rubles per head a month. Of a total of 2,500 prisoners, 300 would be in category I, 500 in category II, and the rest, 1,700, in category III, which had the lowest rations; this kept the average cost of food correspondingly low. If the quota of work imposed by the Labor Department was fulfilled, a prisoner in category I produced an output worth 672 rubles a month, a prisoner in category II, 552 rubles a month, and a wretched prisoner in category III, 373 rubles a month. This gives an idea of the profit the camp—and the state—drew from their grinding work. It also explains, more even than the political side, why it is necessary for the Soviet State to have a huge army of prisoners. Convict labor on this scale is so much cheaper than free workers. Convicts can be sent anywhere, to work under any conditions, to prepare the ground for vast new schemes of industry and agriculture, to open up new mines or oil wells, and to fertilize the arctic wasteland—at any price.

This is not an insight I won only after getting away from the camps and looking at them from outside. The prisoners and deportees are the best-informed persons in the U.S.S.R. They can talk freely to each other as no one else would. Certainly there are informers at large among them, but these are soon found out. And in any case, what punishment could touch those to whom the worst had been done? The hastening of death holds no terrors for most of them.

A prisoner who has been able to resist the crushing weight of his surroundings, who has not sunk into hopeless despair as one who waits impatiently for his death because he knows himself defeated, has saved his inner freedom. In his fashion, he fights on. One of the ways to fight on is to speak to others such as he and to learn what the world is like to which he has been condemned.

A Soviet prisoner sentenced to a long term of hard labor is likely to be moved from one camp to another, following the changes in the manpower requirements of the different places. In each camp he meets many hundreds like him who have passed through a series of camps. When all their information is pooled, the result is a comprehensive view, at least of the world of camps and prisons, often of much more. It was through this network that I learned my facts.

* * * * *

My work as a Stakhanovite propagandist brought me in touch with a woman who, herself deported, was the wife of the commander of two large camps in the Vorkuta region. The reason why she was deported was no fault of her own, even in the eyes of the regime. In fact she was a stanch Communist, partly no doubt because she was in a privileged position and saw the suffering around her through tinted glasses. But her father, an old Bolshevik from the Ukraine, had been sentenced in one of the great purges, and this had brought her to the Vorkuta. By profession she was an engineer. She was young—twenty-four—attractive and intelligent. And she was not in love with her husband, the camp commander.

On several occasions she introduced me to one of the periodical camp meetings devoted to "social emulation," Stakhanovite propaganda and Communist teaching. The last two times she placed me at her side, and said something like, "Comrade Komisaro Piotr Antonovich is of Spanish origin and was one of the heroes in the Spanish War. Now he is a hero of labor in our socialist country. Today as then he fulfills the demands which our great Comrade Stalin makes on true Communists."

I thought that her interest in me was greater than that she might feel in a "hero of labor," though she seemed sincere enough in that. A couple of times we left those meetings together. I saw her regularly when I drew the rations for my gang, since she was the "prisoners' delegate" in charge of food and tobacco issues. Our friendship ripened quickly. From the times of the Civil War she had a high idea of Spaniards, and my nationality intrigued her. She asked me, "Is it true, as they say, that Spaniards are made for death and love?"

"Death and love come to everyone," I answered.

We passed easily from words to deeds. We became lovers.

This affair had great practical advantages for me. Like everyone who had access to supplies in the camps, my friend was running a black-market swindle. The difference between the official prices and the free market prices

made this highly profitable and easy. A packet of cigarettes, for example, cost officially 2 rubles; on the black
market it fetched 30 rubles. The main buyers were officers
and officials who had no direct access to state supplies
through their work. The risk they ran was not great,
because the state did not lose through those deals. The
accounts my friend kept were always in order, everything
was entered at the official price, and the only fact which
did not emerge from her books was how many goods
had been sold at higher prices.

My journeys from one camp to another made me a useful partner for her. Each time they sent me away, I took
with me a bag full of goods she had procured. The gift
of some packets of cigarettes won me accomplices among
the lesser officials on the route. Soon my share of the
profits added up to the respectable sum of 18,000 rubles.
It was the first step towards my escape—the means to
finance it.

I made the second step through another woman in a
key position. The six months during which I was excused
from hard work were running out. I had to go before a
medical commission if I wanted to get an extension of my
state of immunity, which I did. In her capacity as prisoners' delegate, my friend herself prepared the necessary
papers for the doctor to whom she recommended me.
Those papers introduced me as an outstanding Stakhanovite and could not have been much more flattering

if I had been an N.K.V.D. officer. Thus armed, I went to the polyclinic in Kirov Street, the main street of Vorkuta.

The doctor was a young woman in her mid-twenties, with the rank of captain in the N.K.V.D. She received me with the words, "So you are the famous Spaniard I've heard so much about?" and looked me up and down as, I think, only Soviet women look at men. Instead of talking of medical matters, she made me sit down and launched into chitchat. "I hear you Spaniards are crazy about bullfights," she said. "I'd love to see one myself. One day you must tell me what they're like."

"I'm not a typical Spaniard. I don't like bullfights," I answered.

"How disappointing!" she exclaimed. "But I also hear that all Spaniards like women and are Don Juans. Perhaps you don't like women either?"

I laughed and said, "As for that, I am a typical Spaniard."

She went on, as I had expected, "That's better. And what kind of women do you prefer? How do you like me?"

Naturally I answered, "Very much." As a matter of fact, this was true. She was a handsome woman. I seized the opportunity to give her the first of what was to be a series of presents. I have forgotten exactly what it was. She told me that she liked my method of courting and liked me. It was a long session, and she kept her other patients waiting. When I left at long last, she told me to come back soon and send in my name, then she would always see me at once. In this way my lover, the engineer and prisoners' delegate, introduced me to my lover, the doctor.

My rapid success with her was understandable for several reasons. There was the general background. Sexual relationships were treated with a matter-of-fact frankness in Russia. Nobody paid any attention to the affairs of others, nobody felt bound to hide his own affairs, and nobody was shocked if a man or woman had several lovers at the same time. I, personally, had the physical advantage of not looking so emaciated and exhausted as most of the men the doctor had to deal with. Also, my Spanish origin seemed to attract Russian women who craved an emotional force they did not find in the men of their country.

And then, I approached them in a spirit that was new to them. Those women were not satisfied with the unrelieved bareness and coarseness of their relationships with men. The old Russian customs which had been thrown overboard may have been false and "bourgeois"; their elimination may have raised women to sexual equality with men—or degraded both of them to the same level; but the Russian women seemed to feel that they had lost something and expanded gratefully at the slightest whiff of old-fashioned gallantry. They liked to be given presents; they were so touched by a tribute of affection as if they had been starved of it. I was able to give the doctor presents thanks to my other friend. Soap, perfume, sweets, good cigarettes existed in Vorkuta, but in theory they were only for the high-ups above the rank of captain. A prisoners' delegate had access to all these luxuries through the Supplies Department. And this helped me to woo the doctor, as far as wooing was needed.

After a few visits to the clinic, she told me that she could arrange it so that the medical commission would extend my certificate of "unfitness for work." But it would cost money. Her influence alone would not be enough; what she could do was to talk her colleagues on the commission into letting me bribe them. Thanks to my black market earnings, I could afford to do so.

The commission which "examined" me consisted of a major, my friend the captain, and three other N.K.V.D. officers. They examined me with no more professional seriousness than at the monthly examination in the camp. I was through in ten minutes, equipped with a chit which declared me unfit for hard work for another six months.

My new lover obtained an even more precious document for me. By harping on my excellent record during the last eighteen months she secured for me a legal permit to spend four months in the south convalescing after my accident at work. I was given the choice between two cities, Tashkent or Samarkand. I chose Samarkand. From Tashkent I would have had to cross a part of Siberia to get out of the country. Samarkand was in the region I had studied closely for my first escape.

Thus two women made it possible for me to leave the frozen desert of Vorkuta. I never returned.

XVII

IN JUNE, 1947, I started on my journey to Samarkand.
My travel papers laid down that I was to go via Kirov,
Moscow, Kharkov, Rostov, Baku, and Krasnovodsk, and
not to stop for more than twenty-four hours in any one of
those places.

It may sound incredible that somebody sentenced to
hard labor in Siberia was let loose in this form. But the
camp authorities knew the close mesh of the N.K.V.D.
all over Russia, and thought that a prisoner's self-interest
would prevent him from making any step which would
send him back to Siberia with a much harder sentence.
The travel papers they issued to me served their purpose.
At any control, the slightest irregularity would lead to
my arrest. For the same reason those travel papers did
not serve my purpose. A traveler who was not an official
and came from the far north could only be a deported
person, a prisoner or an ex-prisoner, and was automati-
cally suspect even if his papers were in order. Mine would
not always be in order; at some stage I was going to leave
the route of my official itinerary and make my attempt to

[196]

escape. For that stage I needed papers of a different class to arm myself against the checkups and controls I had to expect. In my case, the only such paper was a political refugee identity card issued and stamped at Moscow.

I had exactly twenty-four hours there in which to get it. My other errand in the capital would have been to get in touch with my wife and see my little daughter for the first and possibly last time. I dared not do it, nor even to telephone Ariadna. In the atmosphere which again shrouded the capital—new fear and terror, under the pressure of the propaganda that the "Anglo-American imperialists" were out to destroy the Soviet Union by another war—I would only have compromised my wife and drawn the attention of the N.K.V.D. upon myself. That a visit would not be noticed, a telephone call neither tapped nor overheard, was too much to expect. I did not see my wife and child.

The office from which I had to get my refugee card was that of the Spanish Communist Committee. It was not a good address for me, after my past experiences, but I had no choice. Any other body to which I might have applied would only have passed on my request to the Spanish bureau, and I could not afford to lose time. It was best to take the bull by the horns. I was in luck. Both men who had to sign the card were at the office: José Antonio Uribe, who was still in charge of all refugee matters under the immediate control of La Pasionaria, and Sentís, who issued all Spanish refugees' papers as a member of the direction of Red Aid. And my personal enemies, La Pasionaria herself and Lister, were away.

My sudden reappearance in Moscow caused, of course, a sensation. But they had had reports of my excellent conduct in the northern camps and assumed that I was a reformed character, a new Campesino who was at last prepared to take orders from the Party without arguing. My new technique did the trick. I was subdued and submissive, used the correct Party phrases, and did not let myself become angry. It took some persuasion, but in the end I got my card. It was signed not only by Uribe and Sentís, but also by the vice-president of Red Aid, a Czech ex-deputy who spoke perfect Spanish.

Though I was now well equipped with documents, I took no chances on my further journey. There was always the danger that Dolores Ibarruri, La Pasionaria, would cancel my refugee card as soon as she heard about it, and that the N.K.V.D. commands on my route would be informed. I changed trains frequently and avoided spending a night in places where I would be asked for my papers.

In Kharkov I picked up a girl student who took me to her room in the Scientific Institute. A militiaman stood guard at the gate, but she told him I was her fiancé who had come to see her. Whether the guard believed her story or not, he certainly accepted my offering, two

packets of cigarettes—brand Tiflis No. 5—and a half bottle
of vodka which had cost me 160 rubles. The girl's father
and two brothers had been deported to Siberia. When
she heard that I too had been in the labor camps of the
north, she became very sympathetic and let me sleep in
her room for two nights. She even came with me for a
part of the train journey to Rostov. There I spent another
two nights in a very similar fashion. Precisely because
regulations were so severe, the supervision of trains and
travelers so strict, many people made a living out of cir-
cumventing them and trading on the black market in
rooms. At every important railway station young women
mixed with the crowds and offered the use of their rooms
for a hundred rubles.

From Rostov to Baku I traveled in the compartment
of the woman conductor; this cost me a half bottle of
wine—this time I could not get hold of vodka—a pound of
black bread, a piece of sausage, and two apples. My only
trouble was on the boat from Baku to Krasnovodsk,
where I had not expected a control. But things had
changed since my first attempt to escape. Shortly before
we entered port at Krasnovodsk, a N.K.V.D. officer demanded to see my papers. Around me other travelers'
papers were subjected to a very careful examination. I
feared that the officer would find out that I had already
exceeded the time allowed for my journey. When I
handed him my travel papers, I stuck a few hundred-

ruble notes between them. The N.K.V.D. man moved not a muscle in his face, looked conscientiously through my papers, and returned them to me—without the money. I breathed deeply.

Then came the final stage. I followed the basic plan of my first escape and once again took the train from Krasnovodsk to Samarkand. This time I chose the station of Bamy, about 200 miles from the Persian frontier, as my point of departure. There I got off the train. As long as I stayed in the station itself, I was still on my legitimate route, and even if the police discovered the discrepancy in the dates of my journey, I could hope to talk myself out of the punishment—three years' hard labor and afterward a return to Siberia—which was the rule for offenses like mine in this frontier region. From the moment I left the station, I was a lawbreaker. With an uneasy feeling I crossed the invisible boundary and began to walk through the village of Bamy.

Nobody paid any attention to me. Soon I was past the houses and went on walking as unconcernedly as I could, while I was looking for the best spot to leave the road and cut across country. In front of me the road ran through a little hollow between two hills. I thought I might still be seen from the village if I went off the road at this point, while the two small hills would serve me as a cover farther on. My decision was wrong. I had not gone far on the stretch of road hemmed in by slopes like walls, when a lorry came from the opposite direction. It stopped. A captain and two N.K.V.D. guards jumped out, and I had to show my papers.

The captain scanned them and asked, "What are you doing here? Where are you going?"

I said I had interrupted my journey to Samarkand because I wanted to look up an old acquaintance, a Spanish refugee who used to work in a Kolkhoze hereabouts.

"You've no right to be here," said the captain. "These papers give you permission to wait at stations between trains, but you aren't allowed to go outside. You shouldn't be here, especially not going in this direction."

I tried to make out that I had made a harmless mistake, but the captain would not accept my explanation. This time bribery failed, even when I offered my watch. The frontier police are not as easily suborned as their colleagues of the interior; they are men picked for their posts for this very quality. Also, the captain was interrogating me under the eyes of his men. He pushed my money and watch aside, and jerked his head towards the lorry, "Get in."

While the lorry rattled along the road I had just come, I saw a chink between the side walls and the floor boards of the lorry. Through it I managed to drop first my compass and a little later my small knife. I still carried a last piece of incriminating evidence on me, a map I had drawn of the frontier region, but I was able to get rid of that in the lavatory of the police station at Bukhara where I was taken first. Apparently they were not yet sure what to do with me, for they transferred me for five days to the lockup at Kara-Kala, and then back to Bukhara. At Kara-Kala—which is the training center for spies destined to operate in Afghanistan, Persia, and the other Middle Eastern countries—my watch, clothes, and shoes were taken from me; oddly enough they left me my bag with food, at the bottom of which I had hidden 10,000 rubles. They never discovered them.

After my return to Bukhara I passed through an ordeal I think of as the worst of all. I was thrust into a dark, narrow cell, or rather dungeon. When the door shut, I had the impression of being trapped in a deep well. The only communication with the outer world was the small peephole in the door, which gave no light. I could feel bare, damp soil, but otherwise my probing hands touched nothing but a bucket in the corner. I began to hear small sounds, a scratching and pattering. The cell was full of rats. After a while I heard a gentle, slithering noise. I stepped on something soft which glided away, and cried out in horror. Loud laughter from beyond the door answered me. I dared not search the ground with my hands. It was only too clear that there were snakes in my cell.

For three days and nights I had no sleep. I tied the bottoms of my trousers tightly round my ankles and fastened my belt at the last hole. When the slithering sounds came near, I shrank away from them, but there was so little room. In the darkness I could not tell exactly where the rats and snakes were, until they touched me. On the fourth night I fell asleep, lying on the ground. In my dreams I felt a snake twisting itself round my neck. When I woke with a start, I found that it had not been a nightmare. A strangely soft body was moving under my shirt, on my bare skin, and a second one twined itself round my waist. I bit back an involuntary shout and lay taut. The sliding and gliding went on, like a caress, and I heard small sounds like a suckling baby's. The sensation was more maddening than pain. I wanted to cry for help, but I held myself in an iron grip. It was as if a tight band was circling my brain. Once I let myself go, my reason would snap. Yet after some days I learned to prefer the snakes to the rats. The snakes were only searching the warmth of my body when I was asleep and motionless, but the squalid rats boldly scampered round me all the time.

Once a day I was taken out of my pit and put into another cell for three-quarters of an hour; I suspect that the guards fed the rats during that time, otherwise they would have attacked and bitten me. The worst moment of all came the first day when they put me back into my dungeon after a short respite. I had believed that the torture was finished. When they thrust me back again, I was in despair and went nearly crazy. On each of the days that followed I had the same hope, more faintly each time, and a wave of black despair when I had to return to the company of the dark, the rats, and the snakes. This was the Bukhara method of "softening up" prisoners for a final confession and for the signing of anything whatsoever. The diet to which I was subjected during that time was a quarter of a pound of black bread and a pint of water a day.

On the seventh day I was brought out of the prison and taken to a well-lit room. The electric light hurt my eyes and I had to blink. When I got back my normal sight, I found myself in a soberly furnished office, before three N.K.V.D. officers, a colonel, a major, and a lieutenant. In front of a writing desk sat an exceedingly pretty secretary. All four were staring at me with naked curiosity, as though to observe the precise effect of those seven days and nights on me.

It was an interrogation like any other I had gone through, and the presence of a well-dressed, highly feminine, and attractive woman made not the slightest difference in the procedure, as I had hoped for a wild moment. They started on a friendly note, congratulating me on my share in the Spanish War—a familiar beginning which could not deceive me.

I do not know how the other prisoners at Bukhara had reacted to the snake and rat pit. It had made me see red. I forgot everything I had learned—at what cost—about the need of showing submissiveness to Soviet officials, and countered their compliments with the worst insults I knew in Russian. At this, they dropped their pretended friendliness and overwhelmed me with accusations. These accusations, too, were familiar to me from the Lubianka. They told me that I had always been a paid agent of the British and Americans. Had I not tried to escape once before, with the intention of passing on secret information to my British masters? Wasn't it obvious that I had been caught a second time on the same errand?

I denied their false accusations, as well as the true one that I had been trying to make my way across the frontier. I denied everything, stubbornly and consistently. Then they beat me, not with sticks or whips, but with their fists. They knocked me around, kicked me when I fell, sent me crashing against the wall. Between the blows and kicks of the men I had flashes of the pretty secretary sitting at her desk, calmly smoking and watching the spectacle with the mild interest of a connoisseur. No doubt she would have been surprised if anyone had told her that in some other countries the police had no right to maul a prisoner. She would not have believed it. In Soviet Russia most people are firmly convinced that it is in the capitalist countries that people are beaten most frequently and most cruelly when they are arrested.

EL CAMPESINO

They stopped their work for a while. I was ordered to sign a prepared statement in which I confessed to having been a spy. The penalty would have been twenty-five years in a prison camp. I refused. This time I was beaten until I fainted. On recovering I found myself on the floor, alone with the secretary who was still sitting there at ease, her legs crossed, smoking and smiling. She offered me a cigarette and suggested, in a throaty, provocative voice, that I should sign the statement. Otherwise I would never get out of the hideous cell until I was carried to the common grave.

I went back to the snakes and rats. My daily bread ration was reduced to less than two ounces. When the guard gave it to me in the morning, I gulped it down greedily. During the day I took small sips of the half-pint of water they let me have. For over one month I stayed in the cell. In the end they took me to the room of the chief examining judge, a captain. He said not a word, picked up a mirror and held it in front of my face. What I saw gave me a shock. My once jet-black hair was white. My gaunt cheeks were covered with a lank, gray beard. I looked a wretched old beggar, filthy and degraded, with feverish, madly shining eyes.

But now Bukhara had done its worst and gave up trying to wrest a confession from me. They moved me for five weeks to the prison of Ashkhabad, the capital of Turkestan, and when I was brought back to Bukhara

[206]

it was only to appear before a N.K.V.D. court which took less than ten minutes to sentence me to two years of hard labor.

This was a very mild sentence compared with the twenty-five years which would have been my lot, had I signed the statement prepared for me; it was even less than the usual three years which was the normal sentence for a man from a Vorkuta camp who was detained in Turkestan. The court added, however, that I was liable to an additional sentence if other charges were pending against me in Moscow.

Immediately afterwards I was escorted to camp III at Merv, moved in rapid succession to three different camps at Chardzhui, and finally brought back to Merv. There I had to appear before a medical commission. The doctors found that Bukhara had done what Vorkuta had failed to do to me. I was nothing but skin and bones, not even fit to work in category III. They sent me to one of the death huts I had known from the outside in Vorkuta. At Merv it was called the "dung heap." Now I was not on the downward slope to extinction, but nearly at the bottom. The end should have come quickly, according to all rules of precedent. Yet I still did not want to die. More than ever I had a burning wish to survive, to escape, and to tell the world what I had seen and experienced.

In the "dung heap," I set out to win the sympathies of the chief medical officer. He recognized in me the type of man who never resigns himself to death but continues to fight till the last breath, and offered me a chance to get out of the charnel house. It was a horrifying job he proposed to me, one for which he found very few volunteers; I was to bury the dead. I accepted it. Every night I made the round of the death huts, and sorted out the dead from the quick. Every night there were at least fifteen or twenty bodies waiting for me, and sometimes even thirty.

It was not always easy to tell which of the inert bundles lying on the floor had no life in them and which were only waiting to die. It would happen that, as I bent down, the lips would move and whisper, "Not yet," almost with regret.

I had to undress the dead so that their ragged clothing could be used for other prisoners. Then I had to wrap them in a blanket and carry them on my back, one by one, to the common grave behind the camp. An armed guard and a watchdog went back and forth with me while I staggered along. The dead fell one on top of the other, as I threw them in, like big straw dolls. When one trench was full it was covered with earth and a fresh one was dug.

This task so blunted and hardened me that I came to perform it night after night without feeling anything. Looking back on it, it seems incredible. Could I really have done all that? I did do it. Only now do I realize the full horror of it all. Then, it meant life to me. For the inhuman work I was paid by an extra half ration of bread, ground maize, and, most precious of all, milk. It put new health into me. As my white hairs fell out, they were replaced by dark hair. I was working my way back to normal strength in that gruesome fashion. And this was very nearly a miracle.

After two months on the "dung heap" and as an undertaker, I was declared fit for work. In November, 1947, I was transferred to a labor camp at Ashkhabad, from there successively to five camps in the Nebit-Dag region. After my temporary lapse at Bukhara I had reverted to the tactics I had found so effective in the Vorkuta, and made a show of my good will and complete submission. I was made foreman of a "work brigade," again in the group of Stakhanovites. We were quarrying stone for the construction of "New Baku." My conduct and effort at work earned me a reduction of my sentence by seven months. But then another blow fell. The Legal Department of my camp was informed from Moscow that I had been sentenced to another term of ten years in Siberia, which I would have to serve when I had finished my time in Turkestan. I knew that I would be irrevocably lost once I went back to the north. Again, my mind was obsessed with one thought only, escape.

Meantime I was shifted about from one camp to another, as the masters of the slaves saw fit. In the Krasnovodsk region, I passed through six camps. In April,

1948, I was sent back to Ashkhabad, this time to work in a roof-tile factory. Working and living conditions in the camp were such that the prisoners called it by the name made infamous through the Nazi camps, the "death *lager*." But in Ashkhabad I made new friends, genuine friends. The first was a young woman, a Polish girl who had been a member of the Communist Youth Organization in Warsaw. Her father, a civil engineer, and her mother, a teacher, were old Communists on good terms with the N.K.V.D., but this fact had not saved their daughter from being sentenced to fifteen years' hard labor. The official charge against her had been that she had criticized the Russian authorities. In fact she had not only angered a leading N.K.V.D. officer by refusing to become his mistress and to take part in his black-market activities, but she made it even worse by denouncing him publicly. Therefore she was now in Ashkhabad. From her parents she received occasionally money and food parcels. Even though three-fourths of them were stolen by the camp authorities, what was left helped her through the rigors of camp life. She shared her parcels with me. And I shared my secrets with her. I told her of my past and of my plans for escape. Her disillusionment with Communism was so deep that she promised to help me, although—as she would say sadly—it would mean our separation forever.

At Ashkhabad I also met four old Bolsheviks, whom I

could trust and who gave me advice and help. The greatest character of the four was Nikolai Missa, staff manager of the tile works. He was born in Siberia, had been one of the early Bolshevik fighters, and had helped in the escape of several of the leaders deported after the defeat of the revolution of 1905. He used to say, "Under the Czar it was fairly easy to get away from Russia. It needed Stalin to make an old Bolshevik irretrievably lost in our country. . . . You must get away. You will have to tell the comrades abroad what things here are like. I'm too old. And then, what could I do abroad? Where could I go?" Missa had incredible powers of resistance. He had been in labor and prison camps since 1931. After a first sentence, which he had served to the end, he had again been sentenced to twenty-five years of hard labor and seen the inside of most camps in the north.

"Stalin can't bear to look the old guard in the face," he would explain. "We know him too well. We know what crimes he committed to make himself the absolute master. I shall die in camp. The few old Bolsheviks who are still alive will all die in a camp or a prison. But never mind, Stalin and his totalitarian regime are doomed."

Old Missa could truly be regarded as an enemy of the regime, but his standing in Ashkhabad, even with the N.K.V.D. chiefs, was high.

The three other good friends I found, Victor Ivanov, Korsakov, and Kurgan Amedo, were of the same spirit, if not of the same caliber as Missa. All three had belonged to the old guard of Bolshevism, all three were Uzbeks, and all three were in administrative positions in the camps, which they had won through sheer integrity and energy, undimmed by their long sentences. I felt much less alone than in the years before.

On December 8, 1949, I was going back to my hut in section I of the camp much later than most of my comrades, who were already inside. I had just reached the door when the ground seemed suddenly to drop away from under my feet and the huts began to heave and buckle. A beam struck me and tossed me sideways. A rain of bricks fell. Then, in an exploding universe, I lost track of what was happening. When the turmoil ceased I found myself sitting on the ground, with my head between my hands, and blood trickling down my cheek. Round me was an empty space, and from the ruins of buildings came groans and screams for help.

Ashkhabad had been shaken by the most violent earthquake the district had ever known, and it had come without any warning tremors. At first people thought there had been a great explosion, and a rumor went round that the Americans had dropped an atomic bomb. The press of Krasnovodsk had to deny this and published in proof a report of the Paris Seismographic Institute which had recorded the shock.

My first clear thought was for my friend, the Polish

girl. She and a few other women had been put into our hut, a hut for male prisoners, because the women's huts were overcrowded. I searched for her under the debris and found her half-buried. Though she was bruised and covered with blood, no limbs were broken and I could see no grave external injury. But she was dead.

I was still sitting by her body, stupefied and dazed, when a detachment of militiamen came up. Not to rescue those buried alive under the ruins or to bring aid to the wounded who were dragging themselves about. They turned their automatic rifles on the survivors and finished what the earthquake had begun.

I have no explanation for this massacre. Were they afraid that prisoners might escape in the chaos? Did they find it easier to kill the wounded rather than bother with them? Did they regard it as a useful thing to get rid of people who would no longer be good for work? Whatever the reason, the fact remains: Where a cry for help was raised or a voice groaned in pain, there was a burst of fire and then—silence.

I flattened myself on the ground next to my dead friend and did not move. Near us there were only silent, dead bodies. In this part of the hutment, all had been killed and no one was crying out, so that the bullets were not directed our way. Nevertheless I stayed there for an endless time, shamming dead.

When the fever of killing had passed, the N.K.V.D.

of Tashkent took over and rounded up those who had survived the earthquake and the shooting. There had been 2,800 prisoners in our camp. Thirty-four of us were still alive.

❀   ❀   ❀   ❀   ❀

We thirty-four and the survivors from other camps in the district were taken to Krasnovodsk. There I learned that my other friends were all safe, because thanks to their executive functions they were not quartered in the badly hit prisoners' huts. Old Missa came to see me.

"Go to the camp commander of Krasnovodsk and tell him that your sentence is expiring," he said.

"What is the good of that?" I asked. "I'll have to start on the ten-year sentence from Moscow, that's all."

Missa winked. "All the prisoners' records have been destroyed in the earthquake."

"But somebody is sure to remember!" I cried.

"Everyone in the records section was killed when the building collapsed. Chances are that nobody nearer than Moscow knows about your sentence. It is worth trying."

"It *is* worth trying," I echoed.

On Christmas day I went to the camp command of Krasnovodsk and explained to the commander himself that the following day was the last of my term in camp. Having no files from which to check my status, he telephoned to the Bukhara court which had sentenced me and learned that my term really was no more than two years of hard labor. The camp administration of Krasnovodsk confirmed that I had earned a reduction of my sentence by seven months through my conduct and my work as a Stakhanovite. I spent the next day in anxious anticipation, hoping that at any moment I would be called into the office and handed my discharge slip. Nothing happened. I told myself that prisoners got their release only the day after their sentence had expired. But the twenty-seventh passed uneventfully like the twenty-sixth. So did the twenty-eighth. My hopes vanished.

On December 29, I was called to the camp command. There I received the sum of 14 rubles as a bonus for my work, a loaf of black bread, and a document which said that I was discharged after having completed my sentence and had to take up obligatory residence in Leninabad, Uzbekistan, until further notice. And so I was an ex-prisoner, in precarious freedom.

I walked out of the camp. Missa went with me to the fence, and seemed happier even than I was, though he said not a word when he embraced me. When I had passed through the gate, he walked along inside the barbed wire, while I was walking along it outside until I reached the corner. There he waved good-by and his last look was a message.

But my friend Missa had done me the greatest service

before that moment. He had given me a splendid companion in my final flight for which the time was ripe. Kurgan Amedo had finished his ten-year sentence some days before the earthquake. He was at liberty for the time being, but there was no doubt in his mind that he would soon be rearrested under some pretext or other. An ex-convict is never free in the U.S.S.R. The police regime has reason to distrust those who have served an unjust sentence, and distrust them doubly if they are upright and strong-minded men like my friend Amedo. Old Missa, who had great influence on Amedo, persuaded him not only to help me in my new attempt to escape, but to go with me. I could have had no better partner. Amedo knew Uzbekistan, Turkmenia, and the Persian frontier very well because he had worked in all these regions for years before his arrest. Above all he was a man of unflagging courage. From the day of his release he had been in constant touch with me. Now, when I joined him outside the camp, he brought me new clothes which I exchanged for my prisoner's rags. I felt a new man in them. It was as if these clean clothes, for which I had to thank the solidarity among human beings, lent me fortitude.

We purchased food enough to last us for several days and took the train at nine o'clock in the evening. It carried us past Ashkhabad, where new slave labor had already been mobilized to rebuild the huts and blocks which the earthquake had leveled to the ground. Farther on we slipped off the train and headed for the Persian frontier on the route I had taken years ago during my first escape.

In every respect, the quality of my companion excepted, our cautious progress towards Persia duplicated my former journey. We faced the same problems, struggled through the same rough, hostile country, and took the same precautions to avoid the N.K.V.D. men and their dogs, both more savage than the bears and wolves of the mountains. As before, we walked at night and kept to the mountain heights. Amedo had grown up in this region, he was a mountaineer like myself. During difficult crossings we roped ourselves together. We were well matched. We had no more than two days' journey left to the frontier when we had to risk a difficult passage. Our only workable route led through a small valley between escarpments. By day the N.K.V.D. men might spot us from the commanding heights where they were patrolling; at night, when they took to the valleys, it was equally dangerous. We tried it at dawn, when we could hope that the patrols would be on their way from the valleys to the heights, on the slopes where they could not see us. It seemed the safest time.

It was not safe enough. We were nearly through the pass when without any warning a volley was fired at us. We made a desperate dash forward, but Amedo was hit in the stomach and fell. I tried to drag him along with me. He gasped, "Save yourself, run!"

At the second volley, a bullet pierced Kurgan Amedo's head. He slumped from my arms. I had seen enough men die to know that it was over. I ran. But first I kissed his forehead.

Bullets were whistling past me and tore chunks out of tree trunks. Nothing touched me. I was not meant for death yet. Two days later I dragged myself across the frontier into Persia which, in the changed postwar world, was no longer unsafe for fugitives from Soviet Russia.

I had won my way back into a free life. I had come back to tell the truth of life and death in the Soviet Union, as I had known it.

*　　*　　*　　*　　*

Date Due

AG 15 '52			
OC 13 '52			
NO 10 '52			
NO 18 '52			
DE 26 '52			
Dec 13 '5			
Demco 293-5			